VICTORIAN CHRISTMAS CRAFTS

INDEX

A MERRY CHRISTMAS

VICTORIAN CHRISTMAS CRAFTS

A TREASURY

WRITTEN & ILLUSTRATED   BY BARBARA BRUNO

of GIFTS, ORNAMENTS, AND OTHER HOLIDAY SPECIALTIES TO PREPARE

VNR VAN NOSTRAND REINHOLD COMPANY

Printed in the United States of America
Designed by Barbara Bruno

Published by Van Nostrand Reinhold Company Inc.
135 West 50th Street
New York, New York 10020

Van Nostrand Reinhold Company Limited
Molly Millars Lane
Wokingham, Berkshire RG11 2PY, England

Van Nostrand Reinhold
480 La Trobe Street
Melbourne, Victoria 3000, Australia

Macmillan of Canada
Division of Gage Publishing Limited
164 Commander Boulevard
Agincourt, Ontario M1S 3C7, Canada

16 15 14 13 12 11 10 9 8 7 6 5 4 3 2 1

Library of Congress Cataloging in Publication Data
Bruno, Barbara.
    Victorian Christmas crafts.

    Includes index.
    1. Christmas decorations. 2. Christmas cookery.
3. Handicraft. 4. Decorative arts, Victorian. I. Title.
TT900.C4B78 1984   745.594'1   83-23433
ISBN 0-442-21384-0

For My Mother and Father

☆ ⌂CONTENTS~ ☆

INTRODUCTION

Sugarplums and roast goose, candles twinkling on a lavishly decorated tree, the clip-clopping rhythm of horses' hooves accompanied by the musical jangling of sleigh bells, carolers singing in the glow of a corner gaslight: these were some of the sights and sounds of a Victorian Christmas—sensations that are no longer part of our seasonal celebrations. Other Victorian customs, such as decorating our homes with holiday trimmings, serving special once-a-year treats, and giving and receiving gifts, remain as important to our festivities as they were to those of our great-grandparents. Yet the way in which Victorians prepared for this happy time was quite different from the way we go about it today.

1

In the last century, most people had little money to spend on store-bought goods, and few seasonal items were to be found in shops. Christmas and all its festive pleasures had to be made at home. This lack of commercial fripperies did not make for uninspired celebration, however. Enthusiastic revelers of the last century adapted customs from other times and countries with alacrity. Soberly religious practices took on festive implications under the fun-loving sway of secular Victorians.

Our sociable ancestors were indefatigable game players who invented numbers of activities for enhancing the joys of the season. Householders also found other inspiration for expanding the merriment. Periodicals offered advice on all aspects of Christmas. There were hints on the manufacture of pretty holiday decorations and recipes detailing evermore-sumptuous treats for the Christmas feast.

Friends and relatives gave and received a dazzling array of cleverly conceived and skillfully executed gifts. Gift-making was a genuine form of recreation for the whole family. Directions for creating whimsical as well as practical items abounded in monthly publications. Often the two were combined in a frilled and furbelowed triumph of Victorian craftsmanship. For mother, there would be a silk-lined workbasket with its many attendant accessories—a strawberry-shaped pincushion pretty enough to be used as a tree decoration, lacy needle cases, elaborately wrought wraps for a silver

thimble and sewing scissors.

Fruitpeel flower or scissor-work pictures, patchwork pillows, handmade doilies and antimacassars, mermaids' looking glasses, embroidered wall pouches, carriage robes, and "throws" might lie beneath gift wrap and bright ribbon. A potted primrose or narcissus might be presented by a green-thumbed family member. Father could expect berlin-work slippers, a monogrammed tobacco pouch, a chamois eyeglass cleaner elegantly bound in a crewel-stitched cover, an india-work humidor, or a gift of home-made cookies in a handsome handmade container.

Granny might receive a rosebud sachet, a fragrant pomander, or a "wonderball" of yarn concealing small gifts that would come to light as she knit the many sweaters, mufflers, and mittens needed by a typically growing Victorian family. For the family's young members, there would be a carved and painted zoo's worth of toy animals, a pen wiper hidden beneath some engagingly worked plaything, an intricate, beribboned wardrobe—crochet- and lace-edged—for dolly, or a tiny wax doll in its nutshell cradle, diminutive reproductions of bed quilts, and other Victorian household regalia.

Understandably, planning and producing this cornucopian variety of gifts started long before the holiday drew near. The house was ransacked for odds and ends, and these random finds—scraps of fabric and lace, lengths of silky ribbon, shiny bits of paper, velvet, feathers, and seashells—were

turned, with touches of paint, paste, and ingenuity, into special gifts just right for Uncle Bertie or Cousin Jane. Leftover bits of material from this hodge-podge would be fabricated into exquisite, lacy ornaments designed to dangle alluringly from the fragrant branches of that new Victorian rage, the Christmas tree.

The custom of bringing an evergreen tree into the home had been part of German Christmas tradition for centuries. In England, Queen Victoria and her German prince, Albert, set the fashion, and last century's revelers quickly adopted this child- and adult-pleasing custom.

At first, the tree's decorations consisted of gifts and the candies, cakes, and sugared fruits that enlivened the holiday. However,

it was not long before the Victorian love of knicknacks, ruffles, and flourishes inspired enthusiastic crafters to produce for their trees the engaging trinkets and gossamer baubles that we now consider the epitome of Christmas. Garlands, ropes, and intricately snipped chains of paper angels, chubby paper birds, scrap-work balls, gilt stars, hearts, paper lanterns and flowers, bows and streamers, lacy cornucopias brimming with sugarplums, light-as-air paper snowflakes, and silver tinsel combined in glorious array on the branches of a Victorian Christmas tree.

At the same time, in the kitchen, precious ingredients that had been hoarded in anticipation of the coming event were retrieved from pantry cupboards, measured

and mixed, then baked in the roomy interiors of woodstoves. A parade of fruit-stuffed cakes, crumbly cookies and other toothsome treats emerged from the oven's black depths amid fragrant puffs of steam. This seasonal ritual was accompanied by the longing stares of the household's younger occupants.

The booty was soon packed away in gaily painted tins and salt-glazed crocks and stored in cool corners of the pantry. There the tempting trifles would remain fresh while they awaited presentation at the height of the holiday revelries. Blushing with a pastel veil of creamy icing, stuck all over with chewy almonds, or bejeweled with an armor of bright, sticky fruits, these offerings were sure to arouse admiring

murmers from Christmas guests, while trying the manners of children eager to snatch second servings of the delicious fare.

You can add a bit of the old-fashioned, cozy charm of Victorian Christmases to your celebration by making some of the goodies, gifts, and ornaments that were so lovingly created, presented, and admired in the lamp-lit holidays of long ago. Most of the projects described here need only simple supplies that can be found around the house.

A broad range of possible materials is suggested for each item. You might prefer to use very Victorian bits of lace, feathers, ribbon, braid, or ruffles; but if your ragbag does not contain these ingredients, don't despair. Substitute more modern supplies

as the thrifty and inventive people of the last century would have done. The suggestions here are meant only as a guide and a beginning inspiration.

Craft projects are such fun because, with a little change here and there, you can make something uniquely your own—a one-of-kind gift. I hope that you will have as much fun with these projects as I have had learning about the sights, sounds, and customs of a Victorian Christmas and presenting them to you.

METRIC CONVERSION TABLE

1 inch = 2.54 centimeters

1 foot = 30.48 centimeters

1 ounce (fluid) = 29.573 milliliters

1 cup = 0.237 liters

1 quart = 0.946 liters

1 pound = 0.453 kilograms

HOMEMADE GIFTS:

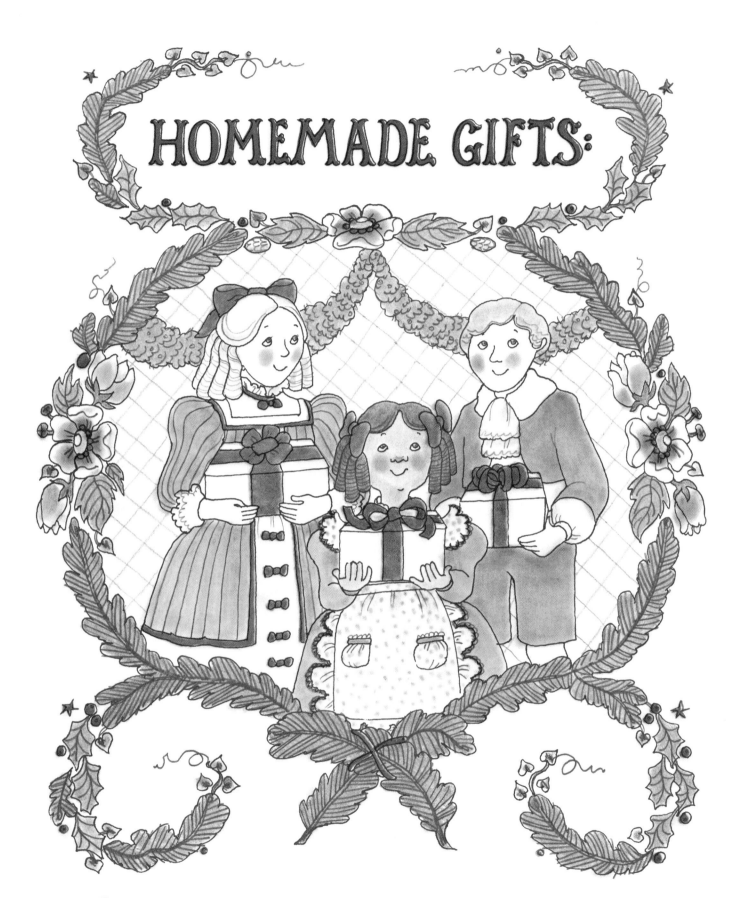

PAPER, PASTE, AND CALICO

Many fine examples of the Victorian skill at turning a hodge-podge of homey ingredients into pretty, imaginative gifts still exist. Some of these presents were practical items useful in the everyday life of a household of the last century. Others were airy baubles which served no other purpose than to show off the nimble-fingered virtuosity of the giver. Such intricate whimsies were meant only for display on one of the army of shelves, tables, and curio cabinets found in most Victorian homes.

Today the faded and fragile mementoes speak to us of a time long past, whispering of rustling taffeta and lace, of patchwork, velvet ribbons, and the incense of cinnamon and cloves. Replicas of these charming tokens so admired by our grandparents would still make fine and unusual gifts, bespeaking of the time and care devoted to their manufacture. Why not create a few of these gifts from Christmases past for those special people on your list?

FRIENDSHIP PILLOW

Handmade quilts kept yesterday's householders snug and warm as they dreamed of Christmas morning surprises. Indeed, every home needed generous numbers of these comforters to stay the chill as fires ebbed during frosty, winter nights. Countless hours were required to make a quilt, so friends often got together to sew the many fine stitches necessary to complete one of these pouffed bed coverings. If the quilt was to be a gift, each person helping might sign her name on a separate block, outlining the signature in dainty stitches of bright thread. These works of art with their quaint embellishment of names were known as friendship quilts.

A friendship pillow made of squares of pretty cloth with the name of the giver emblazoned on one piece of fabric would make a unique gift, just as a friendship quilt did in the last century. One of these parlor pretties, displaying squares embroidered with the names of family members, would be a much appreciated keepsake for a relative, while several individuals might combine their talents to make a pillow for a mutual friend. If you decide to make one on your own, fill the other blocks with the date and an appropriate motto, or use colorful prints for the other squares.

You will need four scraps of fabric, each large enough to supply an 8-by-8-inch square, a larger piece of cloth for the back, pillow stuffing, and a needle and thread.

Rustling silks, velvets, and gleaming satins were favored in the last century. If you have odds and ends of these fine fabrics, your pillow will have an authentically Victorian flavor, but any assortment of plain or flowery cloth will give pleasing results. Solid-color fabrics used for the name squares allow the signatures to be easily seen.

Iron the cloth, and then cut four squares, using an 8-by-8-inch paper pattern as a guide. Names may be applied to the squares with fabric dye crayons or by lightly signing in pencil, then covering the letters with stitches of colorful thread. Allow at least a 1-inch border between signature and fabric edge. You can use either a running stitch, made by pushing the needle in and out of the fabric in a straight line, or a couch stitch composed of small, closely spaced stitches aligned side by side to cover the pencil line. If your plans include either of these stitches, an embroidery hoop to hold the fabric flat while you sew will be needed.

After your name squares are completed, arrange the blocks in a pleasing pattern. Place one square on top of another with the right sides facing in. Sew these two squares together along the sides you wish to touch one another. Use a running stitch or do this on a sewing machine. Make all seams ½ inch from the cloth's edge. Join the other two squares in the same way. Open the blocks and press flat with an iron. Arrange the squares as you wish them to appear in the finished pillow. Be sure that all signatures will face the same way when the cloth is opened. Fold the two pieces, faces in, and sew along the center seam. Spread the cloth. Press flat to complete the pillow face.

Use the front of your pillow as a pattern to cut a square of cloth to serve as the back. Place these blocks together with right sides facing in, and sew around three sides. Turn right sides out. Fill with pillow stuffing. Finish your gift by folding the edges of the fourth side in and stitching them together.

FRUITPEEL FLOWER PICTURE

"The more, the merrier" was the rule when it came to arranging Victorian bouquets. Crowded clusters of buds and full-blown flowers also spilled from vases or baskets in the ornately framed pictures that decorated parlor walls. Some of these floral compositions were painted; many were printed copies of works of art. Others were made from real blooms gathered on summer strolls and pressed in weighty tomes before being organized into closely packed sprays and clusters.

People in the last century also enjoyed creating lifelike pictures of flower bouquets, using such diverse ingredients as shells, feathers, and beads; a most pleasing floral portrait in muted tones and delicate, parchment textures was sometimes made using ordinary fruitpeels. These skins from rare and expensive citrus fruits were cleaned, shaped, and oven-dried before being arranged on sheets of paper to depict abundant, flowery bouquets.

You will need a variety of citrus fruits to make a fruitpeel flower picture. Oranges, tangerines, lemons, and grapefruit provide a range of colors. Add a lime or two if they are available. Aim to keep the skins in the largest pieces possible as you remove the

peel from the pulp. Scrape away as much of the white pith as you can, and rub away the last bits under running water. Using scissors or a knife, cut the peel into all sorts of petal and leaf shapes, varying their size as much as possible. The wider the range of shapes that you have to work with, the better.

Spread your flower and leaf shapes on a cookie sheet and dry in the oven at its lowest setting. This will take several hours, and it is important to keep a close watch to prevent too much heat from toasting them to an unattractive brown. As the peels dry, they twist and curl into all sorts of interesting petal and leaf shapes. When the pieces are completely dry, remove the tray from the oven and allow to cool.

If you do not have a deep shadow frame (such as the Victorians might have used), the lid of a small cardboard box makes a

good substitute—or cut an oval or heart shape from thin cardboard. Use poster paint to color the inside, or glue on a sheet of paper for a background. After the paint has dried, trim the edge with braid, ribbon, paper doilies, or lace ruffles.

Arrange your fruitpeel flowers in a pleasing design inside the box lid, starting in the center with the largest petals and leaves. You may want to use some of the smaller shapes for blossom centers as well as for individual flowers. Seeds saved from the fruit, peppercorns, dried peas or beans, and small pebbles make fine flower centers. Large dried beans also make good flower buds. When your design suits you, use white glue to secure the parts in place. To complete the picture, tie a ribbon around the box edge, adding a bow and a hanging loop at the center top.

MERMAID'S LOOKING GLASS

Because of a keen interest in every kind of natural wonder, Victorians made collecting nature's treasures into a popular pastime. Unusual seashells from faraway lands, colored in the rainbow tints of tropical seas, were given places of honor in glass-fronted curio cabinets. Smaller shells discovered on more familiar beaches came in an endless variety of spotted and striped pastel patterns and were much favored for use in fancy work. These plentiful prizes of the sea might be arranged in intricate designs covering dainty trinket boxes or used to beautify other more mundane objects.

One of the prettier uses made of them was to embellish a frame enclosing a small mirror. This "mermaid's looking glass" was a favorite gift of long-ago Christmases. One of these seashell-framed mirrors can be made using either real seashells or shell-shaped macaroni. You will need seashells or pasta in a variety of sizes, a piece of corrugated cardboard measuring 12 by 12 inches, a ruler, a mat knife, and white glue to make the frame. A 6-by-6-inch mirror and a tape picture hook will also be needed.

An attractive, eight-sided shape was much used for Victorian picture frames. This geometric form looks complicated but is easily made. Measure and mark a point 3½ inches from each corner on each side of the cardboard square. Draw straight lines connecting the dots opposite one another, to form a checkerboard pattern. Turn the square to form a diamond shape before you, and rule four lines to connect the dots that are now opposite one another. Turn the square to form a diamond at the next corner and rule four more lines in the same manner. Cut across the corner lines and remove the middle of the frame by cutting around the inside lines.

Fill the frame with shells arranged in a pretty pattern. Use larger shells for the middle of the design, and outline the edges with small ones. Glue the shells in place and allow them to dry; then glue the mirror in place by squeezing a line of glue along the inside edge of the frame and then carefully placing the frame on top of the mirror. After the glue has dried, tape the mirror to the frame back for a firmer union. Finish by taping the picture hook in place.

POMANDER BALL

Fragrant pomander balls provided a spicy scent in closets and drawers of many Victorian homes. Oranges were expensive, and a pomander ball made from one was considered a fine gift indeed. Today, just as in years past, these deliciously scented spheres wrapped in lace or sporting a fancy ribbon make a present that is both useful and pretty.

To make a pomander ball you'll need an orange, a box of whole cloves, some powdered cinnamon, and a scrap of bright ribbon. Choose a firm, blemish-free orange. Stick the pointed ends of the cloves into the fruit, spacing them no farther than ¼ inch apart. If the orange skin is tough or thick, use the point of a large safety pin or a slender nail to prick holes for the cloves. Finishing one small area before going on to the

next helps to maintain a firm work surface and keeps the release of juice to a minimum. It's a good idea to work over a large shallow bowl or a papertowel; even with care, the task may be a sticky one, but it's always a sweet-smelling pastime.

After the entire surface of the orange is dotted with spicy clove beads, shake the orange in a paper bag with a tablespoon or two of powdered cinnamon. This will help to dry the fruit and to preserve it from decay, as well as adding another nose-tingling aroma to the clove-orange bouquet.

Let the fruit dry in a warm, airy spot for two or three weeks. You'll know it's dry enough when it has shrunk a bit and become much lighter in weight and hard to the touch.

Victorians liked to cover their poman-

16

ders in a froth of lacy fabric. To do this you will need a square or circle of lace about 10 inches across. Place the pomander in the center and draw the fabric up around the fruit. Secure the top with a ribbon tied in a properly lavish bow. Another way to decorate your pomander ball is to tie a length of ribbon around it as you would enfold a package with string, crisscrossing the bright trimming and ending with an extravagantly looped topknot. Narrow velvet ribbon in ruby red or lush green looks particularly Victorian and suggests a holiday mood. Wrap your pomander ball or present it adorned only in its own festive trappings.

STENCIL PAINTING

No proper Victorian home lacked a stenciled picture containing a garden's worth of lush fruits and flowers (often accompanied by a generous number of butterflies, bees, and multicolored caterpillars). It was considered essential to a young woman's education that she master the art of stencil painting. The pictures, called theorems, were often presented as gifts, to be added to the hodge-podge of curios and handmade mementoes so much a part of Victorian household decoration.

Theorems were often stenciled onto velvet, but you can use a large sheet of heavy paper, such as construction paper. White paper works well, or use a creamy tan for an old-fashioned feeling. If you plan to frame your theorem, cut the paper to size.

You will need several sheets of a stiff, thin cardboard called oaktag from which to cut your stencils. Oaktag can be purchased at art or office supply stores. Poster paint and a special stencil brush or a blunt-edged paintbrush are also needed.

Start by drawing the outline of a bowl or basket on a piece of the oaktag. Make the bowl small enough to allow room in the picture for lots of fruit. The bowl can be a

fancy one standing on a pedestal or a simple basket shape. Cut away the inside of the shape to make your stencil.

Place the stencil on the sheet of paper. Hold it in place with one hand as you use the stencil brush to apply a thin coat of paint within the bowl shape. Stroking the brush away, instead of toward, the stencil's edge will keep the bowl's outline clean and sharp. When you have finished, lift the stencil carefully from the paper to avoid smears.

While the bowl is drying divide another piece of oaktag into quarters. Draw the outline of a different fruit on each piece. Cut away the fruit as you did the bowl center. On other small pieces of oaktag draw flowers, leaves, and other fruits. Try the stencils in various positions to help you decide how to arrange your fruit. Those that are to fill the back of the bowl must be stenciled first. Apply the paint to one fruit at a time allowing the paint to dry before going on to

another. Fruits at the front of the picture may overlap those at the back. Stencils can be used more than once.

After all large fruits are dry, position the small stencils of flowers, leaves, small fruits or insects on the picture. These may overlap the bowl or parts of the already stenciled fruit, or you may choose to place some of them at the edges of the composition. Repeat outlines of miniature flowers to make a cluster, or of leaf shapes along a painted line to create a vine.

When all stenciled objects are dry use a small, pointed brush to add extra details to your theorem. Apply bright dots as the centers of flowers, as insect eyes, as seeds of fruits, or as flower buds. Paint colorful markings on butterfly wings and flower petals, or trim your bowl with a flowery border. Wavy lines become tendrils growing from fruits or flowers, or antennae sprouting from jewellike insects. Save the stencils to use again in a totally different arrangement.

What better time to undertake a scissor-work picture than a snowy pre-Christmas afternoon? Comfortably ensconced, not too far from the fire's warmth, yesterday's handicrafter had only to gaze out the window toward the still and whitening world for ideas. Wherever it was that patient and steady-handed enthusiasts found their inspiration, we know from surviving examples that they turned this humble pastime into a means for creating awesome tours de force in the closing years of Victoria's reign: intricately snipped and slit landscapes; birds with amazingly detailed plumage; butterflies whose unflightworthy wings were fancifully netted, pricked, scalloped, and fretworked in gorgeous confusion; dainty, cobwebby networks and zig-zag meshings whose sole purpose was to enclose a sentimental motto enscribed by an accomplished penman with fashionable flourishes. These pictures, as complicated as fine lace, are a testament to Victorian inventiveness and skill.

To make one of these ecstasies of sub-traction you need only a pristine sheet of white paper, a sharp pair of nail scissors, patience, and a sure hand. Your choice of design might be seasonal—a Christmas tree aglow with candles and mantled in a splendid miscellany of decorations would make a fine subject—or you might choose to elaborate on some already decorative creature, such as the aforementioned butterfly. If you have a fine hand, pen a pretty verse and work a lacy wonder around it, or cut out an appropriate example from a card or magazine and make this the focus of your picture.

Start by making a few idea drawings. Choose the best and lightly sketch the design onto the paper. (This will be the wrong side of the scissor-work.) A symmetrical design is much the easiest to undertake, since on the folded paper, one cut will make both sides of the design (although some touching-up will undoubtably be required). Concentrate on placing your design pleasingly and sketching in the main features. Other ideas will come to you as you snip away.

Small scissors, such as the nail variety, are perfect for intricate cutting, and a razor blade will produce fine lines and fringe. Moving the hand holding the paper, instead of the scissor hand, gives more control and is less tiring. Keep in mind that you are not trying to make a lifelike rendition of your subject. Think lacy thoughts as you work. The more unrealistic curls and notches you snip into your cutwork, the more attractive the results will be.

Paste the finished piece to a sheet of bright paper to show off your artistry. Framed, the scissor-work picture makes a unique gift or an attractive addition to your own picture collection.

INDIA-WORK BOX

Inside the beribboned packages exchanged by wealthy celebrators of the last century might be found a gift of rare beauty and painstaking craftsmanship—a jewelry box or humidor made of ebony, its dusky surface intricately patterned with ivory inlay. This ivory-in-ebony work was much admired by all, but beyond the means of many; so it was not long before enterprising householders had devised a charming counterfeit for this exotic craft. Artistically cut paper motifs were temporarily pasted onto boxes of pale wood. Then a coat of black paint practically and attractively stood in for the precious tropical ebony.

When the ingenious artisan removed the paper shields, their pale wood images mimicked the elaborate ivory motifs.

Handkerchief boxes, screens, fireboards, tea and trinket boxes were all popular subjects for this engaging pretense. An india-work checkerboard enclosed in a decorative border is easy to do and would make an attractive wall decoration in a contemporary home. Any smooth-surfaced wooden object will do, however. (For best results raw wood should first be sealed with a coat of clear varnish.) A sheet or two of paper, scissors, rubber cement, and a can of black spray paint will complete the supplies.

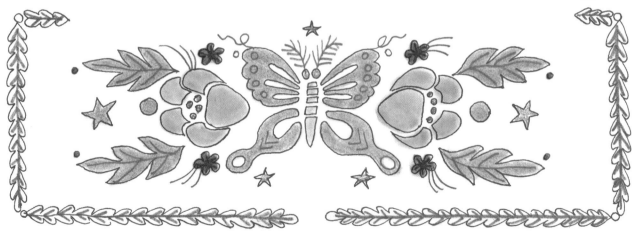

Clear varnish for a finishing coat is optional.

Numbers of paper silhouettes of foliage and flowers will be needed to form the design. Using a variety of shapes produces the most interesting composition. You may decide on an orderly symmetrical arrangement, or you may prefer a random sprinkling of natural forms. Try a few combinations until you see what works best. When you have decided, use rubber cement to attach the paper patterns to the piece. Exercise great care in gluing down the paper figures since sharpness of outline depends on a neat and thorough bonding.

Two or three light mistings of black paint will give results superior to one heavy coating. Allow drying time between the sprayings. Remove the paper patterns as soon as the piece is completely dry; the glue becomes harder to remove the longer it remains in place. The last bits of the cement can be rubbed away with the fingers, or you may use fine sandpaper with a delicate touch for any stubborn smudges. Black oil paint can be brushed on to add intricate leaf veins and other decorative details. Allow ample drying time, then give the india-painting a coat of clear finish to enhance and protect its elegant surface.

BOTANY SILHOUETTE

Victorians were great admirers and students of the natural world. Bird-watching and "botanizing" were favorite leisure-hour pursuits in the last century. Flowers and leaf specimens, trophies of lazy meanderings through blossom-strewn meadows and along the rippled edges of mill ponds, were carried home in picnic hampers, along with remnants of Sunday afternoon lunches. These bits of natural beauty were preserved in homemade leaf presses or sandwiched between pages of the family dictionary and left to dry.

Winter evenings were whiled away in dreaming up new ways to use these pretty souvenirs. "Household elegancies" pictured in the fine-lined engravings of *Godey's Lady's Book* served many hobbyists as inspiration. One way these nature lovers made use of their botanical booty was to arrange airy bouquets of notched leaves, seed heads, wispy grass stems, and fragile flowers, between two panes of glass. When edged with fancy ribbon and placed in a sunny window to cast its lacy shadow, it perfectly combined the Victorian loves of nature and of decoration. Such a natural tracery would look just as attractive in a contemporary setting. Likewise, another Victorian conceit, a candle screen fabricated from a number of these flower shadow pictures and arranged around the light on a wooden base, would make a pretty and useful gift this Christmas.

Ingredients for the silhouette may be collected at any season. While a wider variety of plants is available in summer, skeletonized leaves from forest floors, dried evergreen leaves, and grasses will provide sufficiently varied material for a winter silhouette. Glass may be bought and cut to size at a hardware store. White glue, tape, and a length of ribbon for edging the picture will also be required. Six botany silhouettes, epoxy cement, and a round wooden base with a 7-inch diameter purchased at a craft shop will make a candle screen.

Start by arranging a selection of dried material on one piece of glass. Try different combinations until one suits you. Use small daubs of glue to fix the dried foliage to the glass. Position the second sheet on top of the composition and join the edges with a strip of tape. Victorians would sometimes add an inner frame of narrow lace before covering the tape with a length of fancy-edged ribbon.

Six 3-by-8-inch botany silhouettes will make a candle screen. The back panes should be of ground glass to diffuse the light, allowing the plant shapes to be more easily seen. Make six compositions, each on a sheet of ground glass and covered with a clear pane. Secure the tops and side edges with tape. Join the panels together at top and sides with more tape to form a hexagon. Use epoxy cement to attach the tape-free bottom edge to the base. (You can paint the base beforehand, or leave it natural, as you like.) When the glue has dried, cover the taped borders with strips of ribbon. Place a candle in the center, light it, and admire your handiwork.

Paper-covered "crackers" were staples of Victorian celebrations. No Christmas table setting was complete without these fringe-ended frivolities. The "pop" as the package opened urged on the merriment, but the best part of the ritual was discovering what unusual items lay hidden within the brightly decorated cylinder. The "cracker" usually contained a motto, sentimental, patriotic, or romantic, scrolled with typical Victorian flourishes on its tiny card. Sugared almonds or other confectionary bits and a novel trinket completed the loot.

Although adding a pop to a modern, handmade tube is a problem best left to a chemistry major, you can still borrow this old-fashioned tradition of gift-stuffed favor to provide your holiday meal with an extra bit of fun or as a novel way to present small gifts. Toilet tissue tubes are just the right size to house small knickknacks.

Start by rounding up a tiny gift for each tube, then add an appropriate motto. This bit of whimsy could be comical or could proffer sage advice; or you might try your hand at fortune telling in the style of Chinese rice cookies.

Stuff the tubes, adding candy if desired. Wrap the tubes in squares of vivid tissue, twist at tube ends, and decorate with bows, sequins, and feathers. Fringe the edges in the Victorian manner and place one of these small pleasures at each table setting.

27

PAPIER-MÂCHÉ FRUIT

No Victorian dining room was considered properly "turned out" until the lace or silky-fringed damask tablecloth was centered with a beribboned basket, milky pressed-glass compote, or (in more affluent surroundings) elaborately stemmed and branched epergne. From the treasured container spilled a harvest of everlasting fruit. Rosy-cheeked apples, roly-poly oranges, and more exotic fruits were half-hidden by cascades of royally-tinted grapes—often engagingly fashioned by one of the house's more talented occupants from wax, plaster of Paris, or papier-mâché. This cornucopian profusion of make-believe pommes, berries, and tropical oddities would still bestow a touch of Victorian charm to any décor. Arranged in a fancy basket, these pretty counterfeits would make a fine Christmas gift.

Ingredients needed are few and inexpensive, the main requirements being patience and a few free pre-Christmas evenings. Old newspaper, tape, and a simple flour paste are the required supplies. Powdered spackle from the paint store and tempera or watercolors will tint the fruit.

The inventiveness of the craftspeople of yesterday knew no bounds when it came to furnishing their fruit bowls with mouth-watering variety. Their repertoire included not only peaches, strawberries, currants, and cherries, but a smorgasbord of melon slices and fruit halves, complete with realistically textured seeds (or sometimes the real article was cleverly incorporated).

Choose a simple fruit for starters. Wad newspaper into an appropriately sized ball held together by tape. Mix ½ cup of flour,

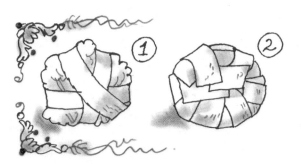
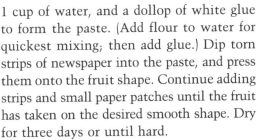

1 cup of water, and a dollop of white glue to form the paste. (Add flour to water for quickest mixing; then add glue.) Dip torn strips of newspaper into the paste, and press them onto the fruit shape. Continue adding strips and small paper patches until the fruit has taken on the desired smooth shape. Dry for three days or until hard.

Small fruits can be formed at the end of paste-soaked, cotton-string "stems." Keep grape stems dry to facilitate tying into bunches. Make leaves and the flat sides of cut fruit by layering several paste-soaked pieces of paper and squeezing out excess paste before cutting the sheet to shape. Leaves may then be bent into pleasing curves and the fruit pieces allowed to dry before you continue to build the fruit halves.

To improve the fruit's surface, mix 3 tablespoons of dry powdered spackle with ½ cup of water and brush onto the bone-dry fruit. Allow the fruit to dry completely before scouring the shape with fine sandpaper. For the finest finish, coat the fruit with white, water-base paint (wall paint works well). After the fruit has dried completely, paint the piece with tempera colors, or for a more delicate effect tint the forms with washes of watercolor. Spray with a clear finish for a protective coating.

To gild the lily, as they were so inclined to do, by-gone crafters sometimes frosted the tacky fruit with a sprinkling of transparent glitter, or a gossamer smattering of gold paint was applied to highlight fruit that was to be combined with somber evergreens.

When arranging your papier-mâché harvest, take a cue from Victorian fruit prints and embellish the grouping with real nuts, silk or dried flowers, and even a frankly fake insect or two. Alternatively, compose a more rustic picture by using a plenitude of papier-mâché vegetables.

Although Victorian householders did not invent sachets, they brought the art of making these "sweet bags" to an inventive peak. Fragrant flowers were gathered and dried throughout the growing season; then spices and aromatic oils, along with powdered orrisroot to stabilize the sweetness, would be added to the mixture. This fragrant combination was used to fill small fabric-scrap pouches trimmed in bits of handmade lace and secured with flyaway satin bows.

A novel and much admired container for such a nose-tingling medley—dainty enough to be tucked among milady's beribboned camisoles and lace-frilled petticoats—was a sachet-filled rosebud. To make a rosebud you will need a 3-inch square of taffeta or a length of 3-inch-wide satin ribbon (in a pretty, flowery pink), thin wire or thread, a pipe cleaner, green scraps of felt for leaves, and green florist's tape for attaching parts and for covering the stem.

Every rosebud requires a teaspoon of sachet. Dried flower sachet or potpourri is available by the pound at many specialty

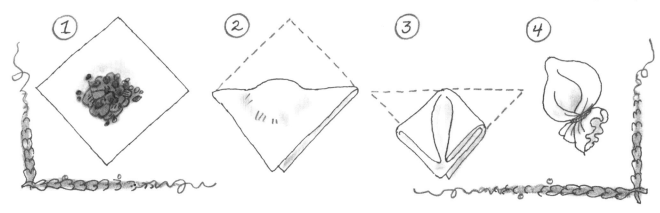

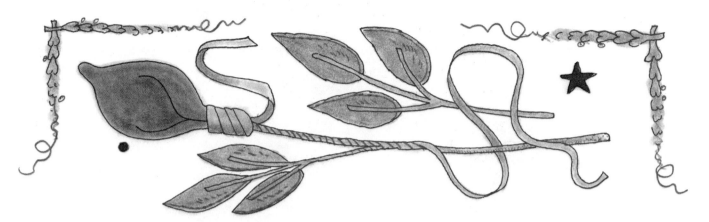

shops, or you can make your own if you have access to a garden harboring old-fashioned, sweet-scented flowers. Rose petals, lavender, carnations, mint, scented geraniums, verbena, lemon balm, and rosemary make a very Victorian combination.

Petals of fragrant blossoms are best picked as soon as the night's dew has evaporated. They should be spread on a suface, such as a raised window screen, where air can circulate freely around them. In a day or two, when they are dry to the touch, they can be combined with a fixative. Orrisroot, gum benzoin, or gum storax are all used for this purpose and can be gotten at a drug store. Use ½ ounce of fixative to a quart of petals. Scented oils may be added to intensify the fragrance. Mix the ingredients and store the blend in a tightly closed plastic bag for several weeks to allow the scents to mingle and mature.

To make the rosebud, cut the 3-inch square of taffeta. Place it in front of you with the wrong side of the fabric up. Position it to form a diamond, and place a teaspoon of sachet in the middle of the diamond. Fold the figure in half, top corner to the bottom. Fold the two outer corners down to match the bottom point. Gather in the flaring sides toward the point to enclose the sachet and form a rosebud shape. Secure the gather with thin wire or thread. Make a calyx for the rosebud by covering the gathered bottom with florist's tape; at the same time, attach the bud to a 4-inch pipe cleaner. Cut two sprays of rose leaf shapes from the scraps of felt and attach them to the stem with a twist or two of tape.

The rosebud becomes a moss rose when it is enfolded in a ruching of finely fringed sepals cut from strips of felt. "Moss" can also be manufactured from frayed green yarn or loopy mohair yarn.

Add Moss

Use felt or

frayed yarn

BOOKMARK FANTASY

Victorian periodicals were filled with suggestions for making handmade gifts, and readers enthusiastically produced and exchanged these pretty handicrafts with great affection and satisfaction on birthdays and holidays. Talented hobbyists transformed humble objects, such as bookmarks, into works of art. Bookmarks were often showcases for Victorian mottoes, and these sentimental or instructional sayings frequently inspired the bookmarks' form.

A hand, sporting an embroidered, betasseled cuff, might bear the adage, "No hands should be idle." A lace trimmed and beribboned guitar might observe that, "Music hath charms to soothe a savage breast." "A little gift by friendship's hand conferred,/ Is often to the costliest gem preferred." highlighted a fabric bookmark, or the same sentiment appeared elaborately penned on the reverse side of a most engaging fish, covered in scales of silver paper and finned in a fringe of multicolored tissue paper.

The variety of forms produced by last century's enthusiasts is impressive. These imaginatively decorated shapes were much too pretty to be hidden away in books and today are much sought after by collectors. Mounted and framed, bookmarks make eye-catching wall decorations, just as they would make unusual one-of-a-kind tree ornaments.

Make a few of these period pieces to give as gifts or to dangle from your Christmas tree. Dated and personalized with the receiver's name, they can commemorate a special Christmas for many years to come. Bookmarks can be manufactured from any glittery odds and ends on hand. Other supplies suggested: oaktag, colored paper, ribbons, embroidery thread, aluminum foil, felt scraps or other trimmings, ink, tempera paints, and glue.

After you have decided on a subject, draw its shape on the oaktag and cut it out. A hand should include an ample cuff, providing room for a motto and properly ornate trimmings. Tint the hand a pleasing (but not necessarily realistic) tone with paint or cover it with colored paper. Cover the cuff in light-toned paper to emphasize the motto to be added there. Pen the motto on the cuff in your fanciest hand. The cuff can be finished in real or paper lace, ribbon, or glittery fabric fringe, and tipped in a silky store-bought tassel or a woolly handmade one. Fill any space around the motto with colorful cut-from-magazine flowers. Add a "secret" message in a hinged heart shape

glued to the palm, in the Victorian manner.

Cover an oaktag guitar in flowered gift paper for an authentically old-fashioned look. Guitar strings of bright embroidery thread can be sewn in place before covering the guitar's back with colored paper penned with a sentiment. Make a many-looped bow for the top and allow a length to float free for a strap. (The kind of paper ribbon that can be curled is especially effective.) Trim the edge of the sound box with gold braid, embossed gold trim from a craft shop, or any festive scraps at your disposal.

Cover an oaktag fish with overlapping rows of aluminum foil scales. Roll the bands of scales around a pencil to give them a slight inward or outward curve before gluing them in place. Each line of scales will then stand out decoratively from the one beneath. Start gluing at the bottom, facing the scales toward the tail. Overlap the scales like shingles on a roof. Cover the head in a single piece of foil. Trim the foil ⅛ inch from the edge. Apply a line of glue along the back, pressing the foil into place to cover the outer edge.

Cut several layers of gaudy tissue paper in the shapes of fins and tail. Glue them together along the body edge, and attach them to the fish. Cover the back with a piece of colored paper, cut to size and inscribed with a motto. When the glue has dried, fringe the tissue fins and tail. A sequin or a dot of glue sprinkled with glitter will serve as an eye. The fish may be embellished with felt pens. Matching figures, glued back-to-back after adding a yarn loop hanger, make tree ornaments.

PATCHWORK COOKIE BOX

Homemade gifts are most beguiling when they come in pretty wrappings. Victorians went to great lengths to provide their Christmas presents with appropriately festive coverings. Last century's clever seamstresses constructed an unusual container for that always-appreciated gift, home-baked holiday cookies. You can assemble an attractive facsimile of this fabric-covered cookie box in much less time and without taking a stitch, by using brightly patterned gift wrap in place of the carefully stitched "floral chintz pieces" recommended in century-old instructions.

To make a patchwork cookie box you will need two or more sheets of gift wrap (choose patterns and colors that look good together); a 21-by-21-inch piece of poster board; 16 feet or more of 1-inch ribbon (the elaborateness of the bow determines the amount of ribbon needed); and two sheets of tissue paper. (This 7-inch-square box will hold a recipe or more of most cookies. Decide if your box need be larger or smaller.)

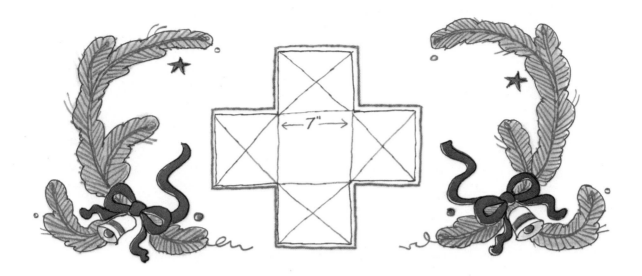

Measure and draw a cross composed of 5- to 7-inch squares on the poster board. Cut out the shape. Crease the four bottom edges of the box. From the gift wrap, cut four squares fractionally larger than the box sides (to allow for overlapping patchwork). Mark and cut the paper squares into triangles. Recombine the triangles in a pleasing pattern. Glue them to the box sides, overlapping slightly if necessary to assure complete coverage. Trim unneeded paper at the sides. Bind separately each inner edge of the box with a piece of ribbon cut to size. Bind the top edges with one ribbon length. (For an extra Victorian fillip, edge the sides with a row of inward facing paper or cloth lace before adding the ribbon binding.) Add elaborate bows at the four corners. Tie into the bows any decorations that suit your fancy, such as silk or dried flowers, sprigs of fake or real berries, bells, or holly shoots.

Line the box with contrasting colored sheets of tissue, which will peek out attractively between ribbon-bound sides at the corners, as well as filling in the box top. Place the cookies in a foil inner lining to maintain freshness and to protect the box from buttery stains.

FLOWER PETAL COOKIE CONTAINER

Lady's magazines of the last century specialized in instructions for turning the commonplace into the extraordinary. One favored method was to trick-out an everyday object in a flowery disguise. Victorians took much delight in these playful deceptions, and the presentation of gift cookies hidden in a giant daisy was sure to inspire admiring comments from the recipient.

Although this petaled parcel is not complicated, it is a project for the patient. A willingness to fuss over the arrangement of the petals is necessary to obtain satisfying results. You will need a 19-inch square of poster board, 2 yards of 2-inch-wide ribbon, string, tape—transparent, two-sided, and masking—and colorful tissue paper. Poster board comes in a variety of pastel shades appropriate for a flower. Choose the most extravagantly pretty ribbon that you can find. A very Victorian and seasonal combination uses snow-white flower petals clasped with a red and green scotch-plaid ribbon, topped with scarlet tissue.

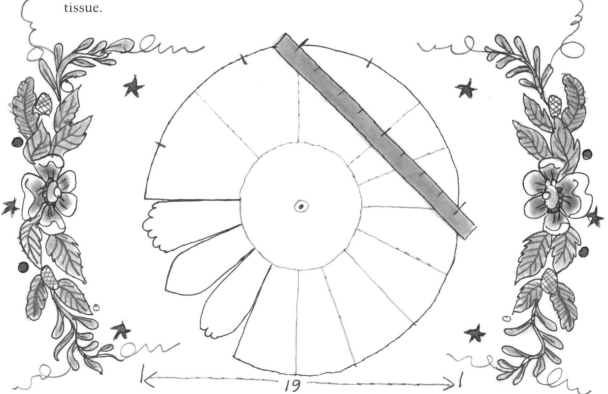

Improvise a compass by tying loops at both ends of a piece of string to make a 9½-inch length. Use a pin to hold one loop at the board's center while you guide a pencil, inserted in the other loop, to mark a circle. Make a second, 4-inch compass and draw another, smaller concentric circle, indicating the flower's base. Divide the circle in half with a line through the center. Divide the circle in quarters with another line. Divide the quarters into eight pie-shaped wedges by positioning the ruler across the points where two adjacent lines cross the inner circle. Mark the midpoint; then, using this mark and the center mark to guide the ruler's placement, mark a line. Repeat again to divide the circle into eighths. Then repeat four more times to make sixteen flower petals.

Round off the petal edges freehand, or use a cup or plate edge as a guide. Notch or point the edges, as you like. Cut out the flower, freeing the petals down to the small base circle. Before gathering in the petals, pull them individually over a table edge, giving them a gentle S curve. Devise a stand to drape the flower over, upside down, as you work at gathering in the petals. A small lamp or shoebox will serve this purpose. Use string or a length of elastic to restrain unruly petals initially. At first, the flower petals seem maddeningly uncooperative, but they can be coaxed to your will.

When you have an approximation of the shape, right the flower and use pieces of masking tape, lightly applied, to help with the adjustments. Lengths of transparent tape will fix petals' positions, when you are satisfied with the placement. Add several lengths of two-sided, sticky tape to the ribbon before carefully placing it to encompass the container. Leave enough ribbon for a generous bow, or add a preconstructed one. Tie sprigs of greens, bells, make-believe berries, silk flowers, or other ornaments into the bow. Line the container with a large sheet of tissue before adding a foil inner lining and the festive sweets.

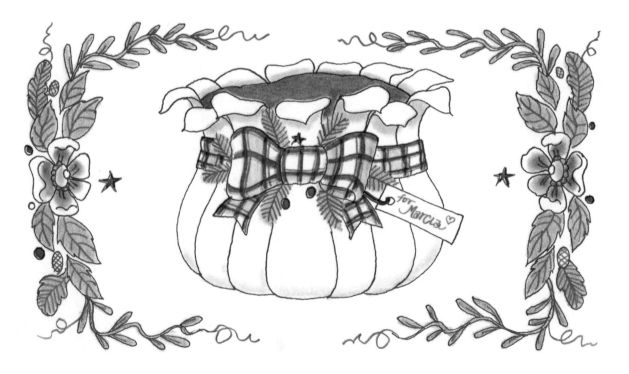

DECK THE HALLS:

GARLANDS, BOWS, AND EVERGREENS

Last century's Christmas celebrations took place at home; and for home-loving Victorians, Christmas was not complete without a copious domestic backdrop of leafy garlands, colorful bows, and innumerable festive sprays of evergreens.

No corner went unadorned in the flurry of pre-Christmas trimming. Walls and window casements sprouted fragrant foliage. Picture frames received holly garnishes, while lace or velvet curtains were outlined with ivy, then sprigged with pressed fern leaves, sewn, pinned, or wired in place. Ceilings displayed criss-crossing green garlands. Stairs required elaborate attention. Long ropes of greenery spiraled down balustrades or descended the stairs in graceful loops. Wreaths decorated doors and hung behind windowpanes, while glowing candles proclaimed the holiday from every windowsill to evening passers-by.

Mottoes and greetings, worked in living or dried plant material, welcomed holiday revelers in foyers. In parlors and dining rooms, scrolls displayed letters covered in gilt paper that spelled out seasonal sentiments, or shields—covered in rich cloth and outlined in laurel ropes—offered best wishes for the coming year to family friends and relatives.

Throughout the house, industrious decorators used a wide variety of materials to provide the necessary festive ambience. Domestic oddments and elements from garden, meadow, and woodland were combined with great imagination. Ribbons, bells, pinecones, and bright berries garnished glossy leaves and fragrant boughs. Flowers, live from the greenhouse or conservatory, forced bulbs and summer-flowering perennials, and brilliant dried blossoms, unfailingly contributed color and scent to the festivities. Yuletide trimmings were enlivened by such diverse ingredients as feathers, seashells, and cotton "snow." Gilt papers and dustings of glitter added their sparkle to the candlelit and lamplit reflections of this joyful holiday.

GREENERY SWAGS

Ropes of fragrant green played an important part in Victorian Christmas decoration. Evergreen swags gracefully echoed the draped line of velvet curtains or garnished tops of ornately gilded picture frames. In the dining room, they served as a rich green accompaniment to a pinecone wreath crowning the sideboard. Green ropes wound around the lamp chain and latticed the ceiling in a criss-crossing network of festive foliage. The swags circumscribed paneled walls of the foyer in elegant scallops, accented at their peaks with profuse bows that might trail silk tassels, bells, or a cascade of the most impressive of pinecones.

Staircases were often elaborately dressed in greens by the mistress of the house. Yards of holiday greenery would be used to entwine each slender banister, while generous ropes traced the handrail's curve. Outside, cords of seasonal foliage followed roof lines or framed windows or doors.

All sorts of greenery composed these lengths. Choice depended on availability and the intended position of the swags.

Laurel, bay, pine, hemlock, and yew were used. For finer ropes, myrtle, box, and ground pine found favor. Ferns and ivies created an airy filigree, while the cream and green of variegated foliage sparkled against crimson velvet or the scarlet flocking of Victorian wallpaper.

The unstinting householder did not stop there, though. Swags themselves were often laced or wound with lengths of red ribbon. Bunches of nuts and berries might accent a curve. Prodigious bows, marking a scallop's end, would sprout flowers, holly, or other shiny ornaments.

Making greenery swags is not difficult; and, once a rhythm is developed, the work goes quickly. You will need an assortment of greens, rope, green string, hand-protecting gloves, and pruning shears. Unplasticized clothesline works well, providing a no-slip surface.

Arrange the rope in the space the swag is to occupy. Short lengths joined at intervals are easiest to work. Allow extra length for a hanging loop at each end. Cut the rope to size. Tie the loops before beginning, so

that they may be covered with greenery. A taut rope is easiest to work with. The swag may be stretched between hands and knees or feet; or make a hook from a clothes hanger, using it to attach the rope to a doorknob or chair back.

Soak the boughs in water overnight before beginning. Cut the plant material into 6-inch lengths. (Fine material may be shorter.) Start at one end of the rope, tightly binding a few stems at a time onto the rope with the string. With stem ends pointing in the same direction, add a few more pieces. Continue, binding the stems securely to the rope. Proceed until the swag is complete.

It is best to hang the swags first, if you plan on decorating them and if they can be reached from the ground. (Finished ropes can be weighty, so large hooks or nails may be necessary.) Spraying the swag with an antidessicant or misting it daily will lengthen its life. (Proceed with care if the greenery is near an electrical outlet.)

MANTEL SPRAY

At holiday time, the Victorian householder's goal was an uninterrupted panorama of decoration. The mistress of the house, aided by enthusiastic young helpers, spared no effort to assure that any unadorned void atop a window or door or bordering a mirror or picture frame received its fair share of profuse holiday embellishment.

A blank expanse over the already knickknack-laden mantelpiece demanded special attention. A "mantel spray" would serve to fill any of these rifts in the yuletide decor. This trimming was easily constructed of dried and fresh greenery, and, if care were taken, the spray could be used for many seasons, provided that some fresh sprigs were added yearly.

To make a mantel spray you will need a wire coat hanger, green-tinted burlap or other coarse-woven material, an assortment of dried and fresh greens, fine wire, needle and thread, and a variety of dried flowers, pinecones, berries, grasses, and ribbons for decoration. Reduce the coat hanger's handle to a small, unobtrusive loop. Shape the wire on each side of the loop into a graceful downward curve, leaving a space between the top and bottom wires. Stretch a few

42

bands of tape across the space to strengthen the form. Cut a piece of burlap large enough to cover and overlap the wire frame, and stitch or staple the fabric to the frame.

Although almost any type of greenery can be used to make a mantel spray, large pressed and dried fern leaves provide a sumptuous and characteristically Victorian background for this decoration. Victorian periodicals recommended that the dried leaves be dipped in melted wax to add strength and longevity to fragile foliage. If space allowed, a few ferns were arranged to plume upward at center, while others were stitched onto the frame following a gracefully down-curving line.

After the spray's perimeter had been filled with fern fronds, small stems of fresh evergreens were used to flesh out the decoration. Pinecones or bright berries were grouped and wired to the spray's center. Boxwood and holly enlivened the design, while long ivy stems were set to trail attractively from spray ends. When complete, these tendrilly elegancies were centered over the fireplace or hung above elaborately curtained windows, providing them with a cornice of rich holiday greenery. After Christmas, wilted material was discarded and the fern and pinecone framework stored for use the following season.

If you lack dried ferns, fresh background material may be substituted. Large, flat evergreen leaves work well, or try spruce, laurel, or any other flat sprays that strike your fancy. Use the same method for arranging the material as is described above. Do try to obtain strands of ivy, since much of the spray's effectiveness comes from this gracefully trailing vine. Be sure to presoak plants overnight. An antidessicant spray will lengthen the arrangement's life.

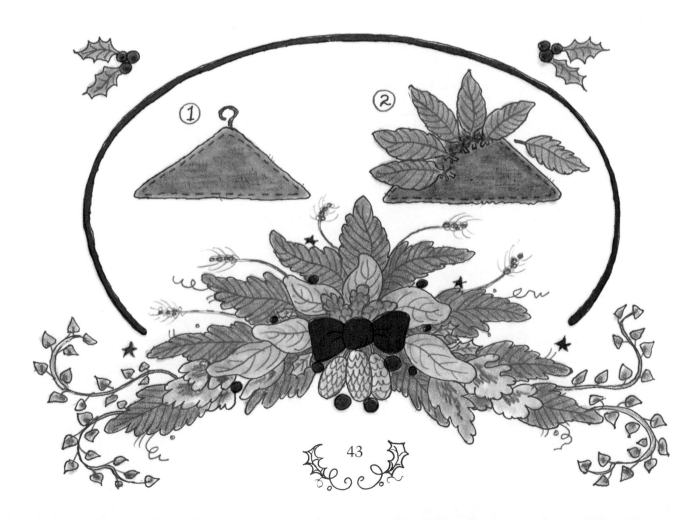

SHIELDS AND MOTTOES

Guests entering a Victorian home at Christmas were often greeted by a brightly lettered shield bidding them to "Be merry and wise" or expressing the hope for "Peace and goodwill" or some such seasonal salutation. Decorative letters attached to a length of ribbon might deck the foyer with the wish for "A merry Christmas," while other similar sentiments hung from the mantelpiece, spanned the parlor doorway, or scalloped the ceiling above the Christmas tree corner. These mottoes were composed of cut-out letters decorated with great ingenuity and charm. Gilt paper, in silver or gold, might have been employed, but just as likely, the cardboard letters were camouflaged with a pretty veneer of dried flowers, ferns, or moss. Sometimes mother's quilting supplies were raided for a coating of cotton "snow," and the pristine letters treated with a glitter dusting before being mounted or strung. Letters composed of twigs were also favored by yesterday's celebrators.

Shields were cut from stiff cardboard and covered in calico, glazed chintz, or colored paper before the seasonal mottoes were added. The shield might be framed in gold paper fringe or in crimped or curled paper. Natural materials, such as dried ferns, ivy strands, and greenery ropes, were also put to this use.

To make a shield, you will need stiff cardboard, glue, and fabric or paper for covering. (To impart a flavor of the past and the look of a Victorian Christmas card, use red gift paper or cloth dotted with small gold patterns.) The shield may be edged with any of the edging materials mentioned above. Cutting the letters from oaktag or other thin cardboard allows for careful adjustment of words, besides providing a firm base onto which you may glue dried plant material or flimsy metallic paper.

Cut a pattern from a folded piece of paper to assure a symmetrical shield. Unfold and use it to trace and cut the cardboard and cloth. Allow a 1-inch margin for folding and gluing the cloth to the shield back. If you plan to use fragile dried material for edging the shield, cut another, slightly larger shield to support and protect the material. Glue the dried plants to this, before mounting the smaller shield on top. Paper fringe can be glued or stapled to the shield's back. Greenery ropes are best attached with a large needle and thread.

If you have a steady hand, letter the motto on the paper pattern, then cut out the letters to use as guides. If you prefer, you can buy cardboard letter patterns or stamped gold paper letters at a stationary or craft store. Trace the patterns onto the oaktag. Cut out the letters. Arrange the words on and glue them to the shield, before covering the letters with fragile dried material. Other coverings may be applied first. After the glue is dry, hang the shield with a loop of thread.

Cutout letters for a motto need to be of stiff cardboard that will hold its shape when strung. Make the motto letters as you would those for the shield. Choose a covering for the letters that will contrast with the setting. Gold paper or crumpled aluminum foil will add sparkle to a dark corner. Colored paper or bright, dried flowers look attractive against wood paneling. "Snow"-covered letters strung on red ribbon look especially Christmasy. Use a thick craft glue for any hard-to-secure material. Tape letters to a length of ribbon or string before suspending them to greet your holiday guests.

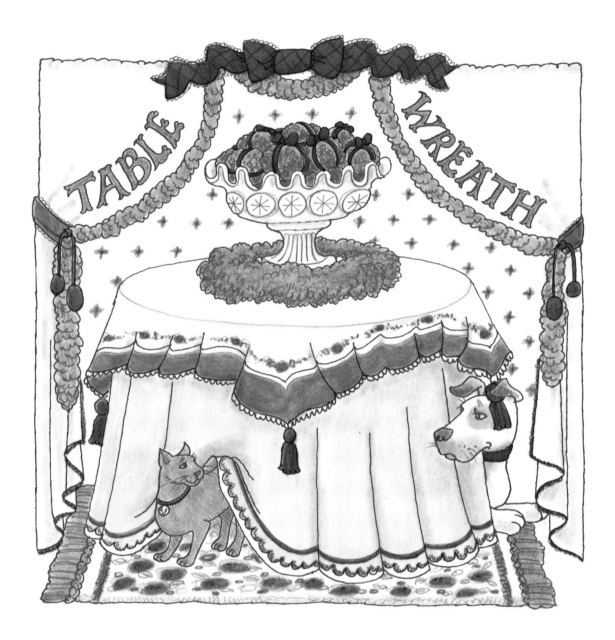

Whether lace-covered or laid with a fringed square of elaborate damask, the dining room table was a focus of holiday interest. In anticipation of approaching festivities, the elaborate container of fruit usually positioned beneath the hanging lamp was whisked away—to be replaced by a handsome display in keeping with the season.

One such popular centerpiece was the table wreath. Ivies and other fine-leaved plant materials were fashioned into a verdant circlet. If the wreath was destined to frame the base of an ornate punch bowl or a footed, milk-glass compote heaped with frosted fruit, plain forest green might be deemed a handsome contrast. For a wreath encircling four fat red advent candles, the arranger might add bunches of red berries, tiny pinecones, silky bows, or other diminutive frills.

Our great-grandmothers would have thought a round, aluminum pizza tray the perfect base for a table wreath. It provides the water-proof receptacle necessary for daily mistings that keep living decorations fresh for many weeks. Along with a pizza tray, you will need a wire wreath frame with a circumference identical to that of the tray, several handfuls of sphagnum moss, small-leaved greens, plant pruners or kitchen shears for snipping stems, and any additional decorations that you desire.

Presoak the greens overnight. Saturate the moss by submerging it in water for an hour. Pack the frame with wet moss and position it on the tray. Press a carpet of moss on the tray's exposed center. Cover the frame with greenery, inserting the stem-ends into the moss and utilizing the frame to hold rebellious lengths in place. Long strands of ivy can be woven into the frame. Keep all stems "growing" in the same direction. Arrange the stems to conceal the tray's edge before adding the punch bowl or candles. You can allow the candles to glow decoratively among a monochrome of shining green, or nestle bright baubles among the foliage of the wreath. Mist and water the wreath frequently; in time, the green snippets may develop roots.

★ FROSTED ★ CENTERPIECE

Choice fruits glazed with a sugar frost and artfully arranged in a multitiered silver epergne reigned over many Victorian holiday feasts. Grapes, an out-of-season luxury, were considered the most elegant of Christmas table decorations. Their coolly glittering forms enrobed in a pretend rime were heaped in polished and pedestaled receptacles, to reside in splendor.

In humbler households, frosted centerpieces were constructed of equally delicious, if less rare, ingredients. A variety of nut– or coconut-stuffed dried fruits—figs, dates, apricots, and prunes—gave interest to the sparkling table garnish. Knots of cranberries and crabapples blushed in mock-icy grandeur. Small pieces of rich green pine or holly inserted here and there among the sugar-coated morsels set off the cool perfection.

Today's variety of candied, dried, and fresh fruits far surpasses the choice offered our ancestors, but the appeal of these natural sweets and fruits dressed in a sparkling mantle has not changed. To make a frosted centerpiece you will need fruit, 2 egg whites, 1 tablespoon of water, and ½ cup of granulated sugar. Choose small, perfect fruit. Pale green grapes are especially pretty, by themselves or with other crystal-flecked companions. Cherries, strawberries, kumquats, and tiny plums are good choices. Dried or candied fruits may be added for variety.

Wash the fresh fruit. Allow it to dry thoroughly. Beat the egg whites and water until the mixture is frothy, but not stiff. Dip the fruit into the mixture, and then roll it in the granulated sugar. Set this aside to dry before arranging the frosted fruit in a container. You can add a few walnuts and pine sprigs for contrast. The fruit looks especially attractive in a footed, milk-glass bowl encircled at its base by a greenery wreath.

Frosted fruit makes an appetizing decoration for holiday food. You might want to replicate the Victorian garnish of frosted holly leaves for some iced dish, such as a cranberry gelatin mold.

★ ★ ★ ★ ★

TRINKET CHAPLET

Victorian family camaraderie inspired many sorts of holiday traditions. One such communal delight that helped to enliven the season was the trinket chaplet. This dainty wreath, suspended on bright ribbons beneath the prismed arms of the dining room lamp, captivated young and old revelers on Christmas morning. At breakfast, its edible and eye-catching decorations could be admired—and, perhaps, sampled.

A cornucopian variety of the most delicate and desired treats—sugarplums wrapped in shiny silver foil, snowy, coconut-topped confections in their fluted paper cups, elaborately iced cookies cut in the shapes of miniature hearts and stars—nestled among a bright collection of lilliputian ornaments. Dangling beneath the circlet, on whisps of multicolored ribbon, were other toothsome morsels strung for the purpose. This rainbow-tinted collection was eyed with special interest by the gathering because suspended among the profusion was a tissue-wrapped parcel for each family member, the first of many trinkets and treasures to delight each individual on that happy holiday.

To make a trinket chaplet, you will need a styrofoam ring, greens, green burlap, wire, floral picks, several yards of narrow,

multicolored ribbon, and a length of wider ribbon for bows and hanger. A goodly assortment of treats, decorations, and special gifts will complete the decoration. A trinket chaplet must be of delicate proportions and slight weight: undue weight should not be added to any electrical light fixture.

Soft and mossy ground pine was the Victorian choice for this decoration. Other possibilities are boxwood or small-leaved holly. A small styrofoam ring wrapped in strips of loosely-woven green fabric, such as burlap, makes an almost weightless base. Attach two wire loops to the ring to facilitate hanging.

Plant material should be soaked overnight before the wreath is assembled. Wire some of the larger sprigs in place, then fill in with bunches of greens secured with floral picks. Although the wreath should be well-covered in greenery, perfection is not

required. Small decorations can be used to camouflage gaps.

Hanging the chaplet in its allotted spot before decorating it will produce the best results. Suspend it from the fixture with a length of ribbon, adding a bow at each wire loop. The choice of decorations depends on individual taste. Traditional Christmas ornaments might glitter alone or be joined by shiny berries, nuts, small toys, and holiday candy. Homemade fancies could tempt the eye and palate. Use floral picks in placing the ornaments, when necessary. Balance the weight of the decorations as you work.

Cut the narrow ribbon into assorted lengths—6 inches and less work well. Attach a trinket or candy to one ribbon end. Use a floral pick to attach the other end to the chaplet. Suspend small beribboned gifts to start your own Christmas morning tradition, or add tiny pretend gifts.

A mistletoe kissing bunch heightened the merriment of a Victorian Christmas. Even though mistletoe's magical potency was discounted, the plant still inspired good-natured mischief among family familiars. Young ladies were known to frequent its vicinity, there to be caught "unawares" by admiring swains. Aunts and uncles, grandparents and wee tots all joined in a jovial pucker beneath its pale berries.

Given the past century's unswerving devotion to embellishment, such a delightful tradition was not long allowed to continue unadorned. Encircled in aromatic greens and topped with an imposing red satin bow, the kissing bunch became a kissing ball. Doubly decorated and set to dangle in a position of prominence, it doubly enlivened the holiday proceedings.

For a kissing ball, you will need mistletoe, ribbon, two hoops, finely textured greens, and wire. Though not essential, a handful of sphagnum moss will grant greenery a longer life. The hoops may be manufactured from natural materials, such as willow wands, honeysuckle, or grape vines. Other possi-

52

bilities are embroidery hoops or coat hangers shaped into circles and wrapped with florist's tape to provide a no-slide surface. The hoops should be the same size, big enough to encircle the mistletoe bouquet, yet not so large as to interfere with doorway traffic. Keep in mind that the greens will increase the width of the hoops.

Fine-textured greenery makes the most attractive kissing ball. Choose small-leaved box or holly. Softly lacy ground pine, sometimes available at florists, is a most Victorian choice. Glossy, miniature ivies also give a pleasing period look to the decoration.

Soak all material overnight in warm water to harden it. Form two identical circles and secure them with wire. Wad and tightly wire wet sphagnum moss to the frame. Start at the bottom juncture of the hoops, if you are working with short lengths of greens. Wire a few sprigs in place, stem ends up. Overlap more sprigs, as for greenery ropes, wiring them in place as you go. Continue until the top is reached; then repeat for the remaining hoop ribs.

Long strands of ivy are better attached to the top of the ball, the stems wound round the hoop, and then secured in place with wire. Any bare spots can be filled in with shorter lengths.

After the hoops are completely covered with living green, a thorough dousing with water will improve the longevity of the plant material. Suspend the mistletoe within the framework. Top the ball with a splendidly looped bow; and, if you wish, suspend an equally fancy twin beneath it. To assure optimum merriment, attach the kissing ball by wire at a place where pedestrians are sure to pass. Mist the ball with water daily to keep it fresh.

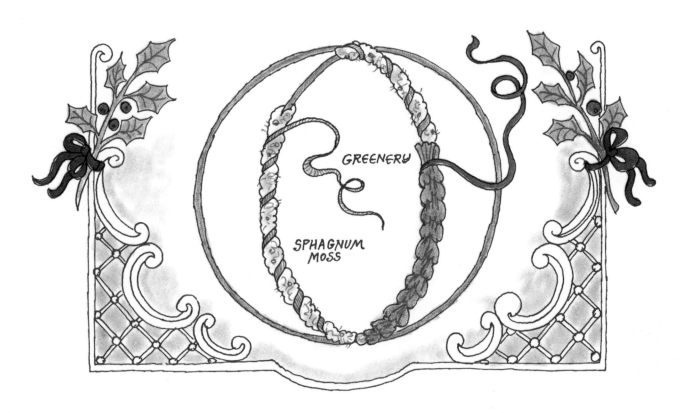

GREENERY

SPHAGNUM MOSS

The first stockings "hung by the chimney with care" were those worn on less festive occasions by the children themselves. It was not long, however, before last century's needlewomen applied their imagination and skill to this holiday tradition. To the younger set's delight, Christmas stockings metamorphosed into roomy sacks capacious enough for a profusion of engaging trifles. Painted toy soldiers, tin flutes and drums, animated penny banks, wheeled and wooly string-toy sheep, wooden horses, candy canes, diminutive dollies, jacks and jump-ropes, cleverly constructed pencil boxes—who could guess what might fill the bulging stocking?

These unsubtle pleas for Santa's generosity grew in attractiveness as well as in bulk. Skillful seamstresses transformed once-humble foot wrappings into fancywork epitomes of Victorian Christmas spirit. Some stockings were knitted of gaily colored yarn and topped with a ribbon ruching. Another typically Victorian design was made of red wool, jauntily cuffed in a jester's ruff of rich green, with each point sporting a shiny bell.

To create a facsimile of this Christmas stocking, you will need a large paper bag, red and green felt, a needle and red thread, contrasting embroidery floss, and eight bells. Draw an 18-inch-long stocking pattern on an opened-out paper bag. Use the pattern to cut out two stocking shapes from the red felt. Cut a decorative heel and toe shape from the stocking pattern. Use these pieces as guides in cutting two heel and two toe pieces from green felt. Stitch the heels

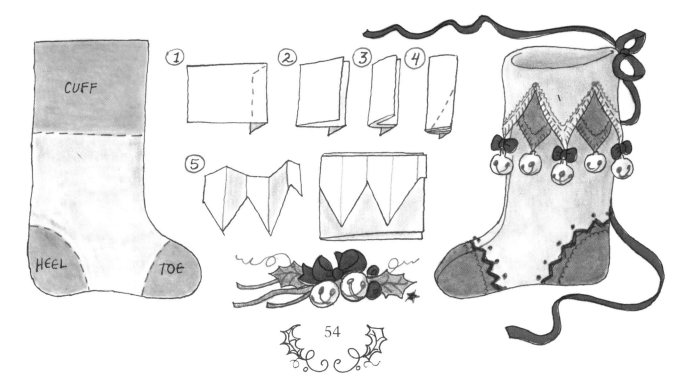

and toes in place on the two stocking sides. Large running stitches or cross-stitches of embroidery floss in a contrasting color will do the job most decoratively. Join the stocking's two pieces, right sides facing in, with a ¼-inch seam.

Cut a pattern for a deep cuff. Make the cuff one-third the length of the stocking. The cuff's width should be ¼ inch less than the width of the stocking's top, to allow for the stocking's second seam. To make perfectly matched points along the cuff's edge, first allow for a seam by folding ¼ inch under along one side. Fold the remaining paper in half, then in half again. Cut a deep, slanting line to make a point at the pattern's edge. (The opened pattern will have two identical points.) Cut a cuff with four points by placing one edge of the pattern on a fold of cloth; then cut a second cuff.

Seam the open edges of the cuff and press flat. Place one cuff inside the other, seam sides out. Center the bottom points between the top points. Join the inside-out cuff and stocking along the top edge. (The top seam will be on the outside, concealed by the cuff.) Turn the stocking right side out. Sew a bell onto each point. Add a sturdy hanging loop to complete the stocking.

55

DECORATING THE TREE:

TINSEL, LACE, AND HOMEMADE TRINKETS

Victorian Christmas was not complete without a lavishly decorated tree. These fragrant fountains of green were enthroned in the best parlor and adorned in a profuse curtain of the most beautiful, most novel, and tastiest trinkets that the household could buy or invent. Trees of the wealthy were draped in yards of silver tinsel before being hung with light-as-a-feather glass bubbles tinted in a dozen bird-of-paradise hues.

These expensively bedecked Christmas symbols were no more attractive than the trees lovingly trimmed in hand-crafted decorations by those of lesser means. Wound round with a scarf of joyfully colored, homemade fancies of every imaginable kind and rimmed in the gentle light of countless candles, these more humbly attired trees attested to hours of happy clipping, pasting, and stringing. These tasks were enthusiastically undertaken by all ages. Working in warm circles of lamplight, they shared a pleasant companionship as the store of brightly colored baubles grew.

It was unthinkable in both rich and poor households to consider the job of trimming complete until an abundance of tasty morsels had been placed among the multiform, multicolored ornaments already crowding the branches. Whimsical chocolate soldiers, rare bunches of raisins still firmly clinging to

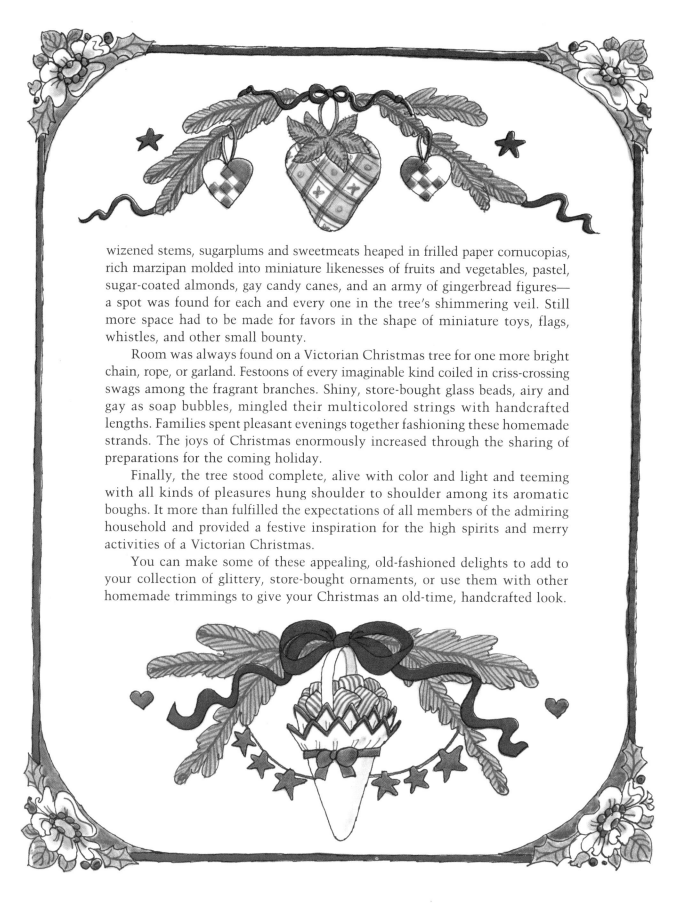

wizened stems, sugarplums and sweetmeats heaped in frilled paper cornucopias, rich marzipan molded into miniature likenesses of fruits and vegetables, pastel, sugar-coated almonds, gay candy canes, and an army of gingerbread figures— a spot was found for each and every one in the tree's shimmering veil. Still more space had to be made for favors in the shape of miniature toys, flags, whistles, and other small bounty.

Room was always found on a Victorian Christmas tree for one more bright chain, rope, or garland. Festoons of every imaginable kind coiled in criss-crossing swags among the fragrant branches. Shiny, store-bought glass beads, airy and gay as soap bubbles, mingled their multicolored strings with handcrafted lengths. Families spent pleasant evenings together fashioning these homemade strands. The joys of Christmas enormously increased through the sharing of preparations for the coming holiday.

Finally, the tree stood complete, alive with color and light and teeming with all kinds of pleasures hung shoulder to shoulder among its aromatic boughs. It more than fulfilled the expectations of all members of the admiring household and provided a festive inspiration for the high spirits and merry activities of a Victorian Christmas.

You can make some of these appealing, old-fashioned delights to add to your collection of glittery, store-bought ornaments, or use them with other homemade trimmings to give your Christmas an old-time, handcrafted look.

POPCORN AND CRANBERRY ROPES

Popcorn and cranberry ropes have been a tradition as long as there have been Christmas trees in America. (Cranberries and popcorn are native to this country.) Their popularity can be traced to the Christmasy appeal of snow-white popcorn and candy-red berries wreathing dark green branches.

Pop plenty of corn for your ropes. You will find a lot disappearing as you string and munch away. Use a large needle and heavy thread. A button tied to the string end will serve as a top. Prevent tangling by using 3-foot lengths of thread, adding more when the first piece is almost filled. Strings no longer than 6 feet are easiest to handle and less apt to snag as you arrange them on the tree. String popcorn and cranberries separately or mix them for a pretty, two-colored chain.

59

DOLLY CHAINS

Chains of dainty paper dollies snipped from thin sheets of paper in snow-flake white or sugary, fairy-tale colors can add a lacy, old-fashioned look to your Christmas tree. Victorian children used sharp scissors to cut the intricate notches and fringes needed to impart to their garlands of dancing figures a light and airy grace as they curtsied and swayed from bough to fragrant bough.

Sheets of lightweight typing paper work well for confecting these gay, smiling ladies. Fold several sheets in half, lengthwise, then cut the papers in half along the folds. Make a four-part accordian pleat by folding one strip in half lengthwise, then folding the two ends back in opposite directions to line up with the first fold. Carefully fold the paper in half once more to form a tall, narrow strip. The folds must match perfectly for best results.

Draw the outline of half a figure touching both edges of the paper. Cut out the figure, taking care to leave some connecting paper along the sides. When the paper is unfolded you will have a chain of four symmetrical figures. Fold another piece of paper in the same way. Use the refolded figures to trace a pattern, or draw a different figure for the second length of your chain. Cut several more strings of dollies. If they do not look fancy enough, add extra cuts before gluing them together to form one long, lacy chain. Arrange the dolly chain on the Christmas tree so that the figures waltz merrily from branch to branch.

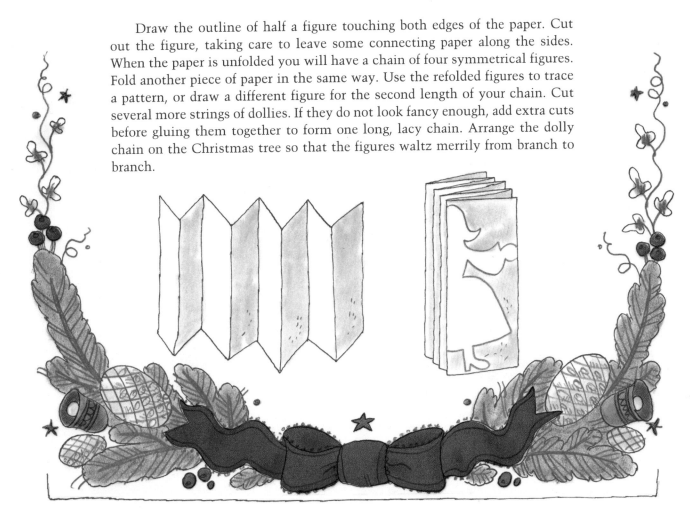

RAINBOW PAPER GARLANDS

Chains composed of entwined paper circles have wound ribbons of color around countless Christmas trees. The Victorian love of frills encouraged taking this quaint decoration a step farther. Using the classic chain idea, they festooned their holiday trees in rainbow-hued garlands of cleverly folded and joined geometric shapes. Sometimes they combined these forms that were made of narrow paper strips, both shiny and plain, to create opulent, looped shapes—butterfly wreaths that wrapped the tree in cobwebby chains of multicolored paper ribbons.

To make rainbow paper garlands, you will need colored paper, a ruler and pencil, sharp scissors, and glue. Construction paper or shiny wrap works well. Vividly printed, glossy magazine pages, glued back-to-back, make gay, confetti-toned swags. Choose light, bright colors to contrast with the somber green branches. Measure and cut strips ½ by 5 inches. Exact dimensions are unimportant, but the narrower the strips, the more graceful the garlands.

Several different geometric-figured garlands can be made by creasing the strips in various patterns. Fold two different-colored strips in half, then fold out the ends, then glue end-tabs together to make a diamond shape. Create a

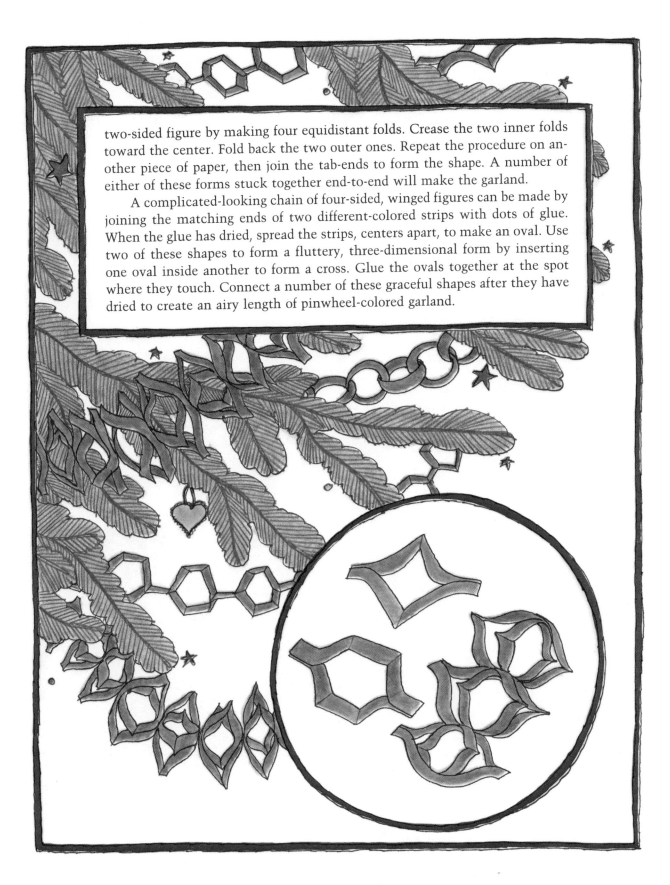

two-sided figure by making four equidistant folds. Crease the two inner folds toward the center. Fold back the two outer ones. Repeat the procedure on another piece of paper, then join the tab-ends to form the shape. A number of either of these forms stuck together end-to-end will make the garland.

A complicated-looking chain of four-sided, winged figures can be made by joining the matching ends of two different-colored strips with dots of glue. When the glue has dried, spread the strips, centers apart, to make an oval. Use two of these shapes to form a fluttery, three-dimensional form by inserting one oval inside another to form a cross. Glue the ovals together at the spot where they touch. Connect a number of these graceful shapes after they have dried to create an airy length of pinwheel-colored garland.

STAR AND HEART STRINGS

Star and heart strings are another old-time Christmas tree garland created from the simplest of supplies. These buoyant lengths could be manufactured by even the younger family members, and they added variety to other home-made swags decorating the tree.

To make a star and heart string, you will need a ball of knitting yarn, colored paper, scissors, and glue. Draw a 1¾-inch pattern of a heart and another of a star. Fold a piece of colored paper in half. Place the pattern on the paper so that the fold will serve as a hinge. Draw and cut out a heart shape. Hang the heart from a length of yarn, adding a daub of glue to hold the heart in place. Cut out a star from a folded sheet and add it to the string in the same way. Continue cutting and gluing hearts and stars until the string is complete.

Alternate the hearts and stars or make separate strings of each. Strings may be multicolored or planned to suit a particular color scheme. Silver or gold paper produces showy results, while wrapping paper printed in a petite golden pattern supplies an appealingly old-fashioned look.

WOVEN PAPER HEARTS

The heart was a familiar and sentimental favorite among the myriad motifs used in Victorian arts and crafts. This symbol of affection appeared in many forms among the Christmas tree's colorful bounty. Store-bought hearts—airy confections of tinsel and glass, stamped tin, or pressed metallic paper—shared fragrant branches with handcrafted creations. Red and white paper hearts were one such homemade decoration. Woven according to an age-old folk art pattern, their brightly checkered simplicity added bold color to the holiday scheme.

Red and white paper and scissors are the only supplies needed for this craft. Lightweight paper makes the most delicate decoration. Cut a 2-by-6-inch rectangle from a white paper sheet. Fold it in half to make a 2-by-3-inch shape. Round off the side opposite the fold. This will be one lobe of the heart. Cut a matching shape from red paper.

Lightly mark ½-inch spaces along one folded edge. Place one piece on top of the other, matching the edges. Holding the pieces together, cut a 2-inch-long slit at each mark. Weave the tabs of each lobe together to form a checker-patterned heart. Hang the heart with a length of thin ribbon threaded through a punched hole and tied in a bow.

Red and white is the traditional combination for woven paper hearts, but Victorian hobbyists occasionally varied the color. They also created interest by varying the heart size and the number of slits, and by using metallic papers. Today we might use small print wrapping paper and plaid or flowered ribbon for a pretty patchwork effect. Just be sure to choose bright or pastel colors to contrast with rich evergreen.

No Victorian Christmas tree was complete without a generous number of cone-shaped cornucopias hanging from its ornament-laden branches. These "horns of plenty" were often made from shiny silver or gold paper, edged with lacy paper doilies, and filled with all the sweet holiday treats that children love best. Cut-outs of Santa Claus, colored tissue paper ruffles, and bits of fancy ribbon were also used to decorate these symbols of Christmas abundance.

To make a cornucopia, you will need a piece of pretty paper, a staple gun or paste, and trimmings. If you don't have any silver or gold paper, brightly colored glossy paper, gift wrap, or white paper decorated with tempera paints would work as well.

Cut an 8-by-12-inch rectangle. Measure and mark the center on one 8-inch side. Place the point of a compass on the center

66

mark and draw an arc at the other end of the paper that goes off the edge of the paper and then returns to it. (If you haven't a compass, tie a string around a pencil, hold the end of the string at the mark, and adjust the length until the pencil touches the other end of the paper when the string is held taut. Let the string guide the pencil as you draw a curving line.) Draw two straight lines connecting the center mark with the spots where the arc touches the paper's edges. Cut out this triangular shape. Cut a strip of paper ½ by 8 inches for a handle.

Form the cone-shaped cornucopia by slightly overlapping the two straight sides and stapling or gluing them in place. Decorate your cornucopia with any of the materials mentioned above or with any other fancy items that you choose. Use rick-rack or other dress decorations, silver stars or letters, pictures clipped from magazines, tinsel, sequins, sparkles, tassels, or lace.

Victorians filled their cornucopias with candy, but you could use minature Christmas balls or tiny pinecones in their place. These "horns of plenty," handcrafted in a variety of sizes and colors, can give your tree nostalgic charm.

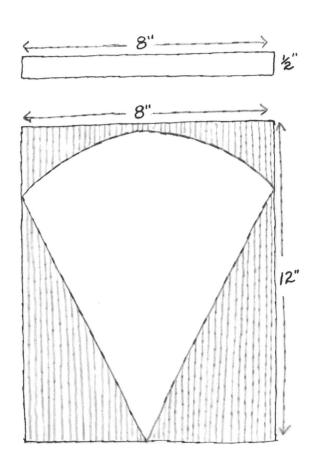

PAPER FANS

Victorians made these little pleated fans by the dozens. The ornaments looked as gay as fluttering birds winging among the somber green of candlelit branches. They would look just as pretty on a contemporary tree.

Paper fans are easily made in minutes by folding and snipping. Pick any paper that suits your fancy. If you plan to make an intricately cut fan, a plain, pastel color will show off the lacy design. Flowery printed wrapping paper notched in a bold cutout pattern makes equally pretty fans.

Although fans can be any size, a piece of paper measuring 4½ by 20 inches is a good size to start with. Fold the paper accordian fashion, starting at a narrow end. Make the folds about ¾ inch apart. Cut out notches from the folded edges in the shape of triangles, half hearts, and a variety of other forms. Use lots of different sized and shaped cuts. The more cut away, the more delicate your fan will appear. But be sure to leave uncut areas along both edges to hold

the fan together. After you have finished cutting, the fan can be opened out flat and some of the notches outlined with colored pen, or let the lacy filigree be the fan's only decoration.

Other fans can be larger or smaller, brightly colored or delicately lacy. Make them with narrow folds, with real lace or feather edgings. Use sequin sprinkles, or weave ribbon through specially cut notches. Cut paper strips and glue them together to create fans with rainbow-colored pleats, or glue on a flowered paper border before folding and snipping. Add silver stars, pressed flowers, or shiny magazine cutouts.

Secure the folded fan bottom with a staple. Stretch the top into an open position. Attach a brightly colored bow to the handle. These airy fripperies are so pretty and easily made that they might serve as a tree's sole decorations with enchanting results.

PAPER SNOWFLAKES

Delicate paper snowflakes suspended among more earthbound baubles set Victorian children's thoughts flashing down crystalline slopes, gliding on the flourishes of opulent paint and gracefully wrought metal that was a nineteenth century sled. Make some of these ethereal flakes to twist lightly at the ends of your tree's branches and commemorate past winters' joys.

You will need sheets of thin, white paper, sharp scissors, glue, and a stapler. Trim the paper to measure 11 by 5 inches. Mark the paper at ½-inch intervals along the 11-inch side. Use the marks as guides to fold the paper, accordion fashion. Staple the center point of the paper, with the staple's longest dimension running across the paper strip. Notch the sides of the strip with a variety of deep and shallow, curved and straight cuts. Match the notches above and below the staple to create a symmetrically patterned snowflake. Open the sides of the ornament and glue the ends together to form a circle. Make a hanger by tying a loop of string through a notch.

SCRAP-WORK BALLS

Paper was not always as plentiful as it is today. In the last century, cheerfully colored scraps were hoarded for use in the endless variety of fancywork baubles fashioned and cherished by children and their older relatives alike. One clever bit of handiwork made from these odds and ends of gaily hued paper was the scrap-work ball. These geometric wonders added a spherical variety to the profuse drapery of homemade ornaments on the well-furnished Victorian Christmas tree.

To make a scrap-work ball, you will need 20 circles cut from any colored paper that suits your fancy—wrapping paper, old Christmas cards, or shiny, kaleidoscope-bright magazine pages. A circular-topped container, (such as a cup) that is about 3½

inches across makes a good tracing pattern.

A cardboard triangle will form a template to guide you in folding the circle's edges. Make the triangular guide by first cutting a 3½-inch cardboard circle. Use a ruler to measure and mark a 3-inch line beginning and ending along the edge. Repeat twice more to form a triangle. Cut out the shape. Place it on top of a circle. Fold up the three crescents of paper extending beyond the triangle.

When all the circles are folded, glue a crescent of one circle to that of another, matching the edges perfectly. Continue until all crescents are joined, with the circles forming a ball. Insert a loop of string between the last pair of edges before gluing, to make a hanger.

BIRD IN A GILDED CAGE

Victorians believed in gilding the lily, and "the fancier, the better" was their motto when it came to Christmas tree ornaments, too. A favored finishing touch to many already lavishly decorated commercial baubles was a glittering veil of gold net. Not to be outdone, handcrafters devised an ingeniously cut web of gleaming, golden paper to stand in for the commercial product. By placing a paper songster inside the bright mesh, they created a bird in a gilded cage.

To make this ornament you will need sharp scissors, shiny gift wrap, colored paper, glue, and a needle and thread. The wrap need not be gold-colored. Any metallic shade will do, but choose a lightweight one, since many layers must be snipped through at once. Cut an 8-inch square. Fold the figure in half, then in half again to form a 2-inch square. From the corner of the square that was the paper's center, fold the figure diagonally to make a triangle. Make all

creases as nearly perfect as possible, since precise folds give the best results.

Mark the center of the triangle's long side. Make a straight cut from the mark toward the opposite corner, leaving ¼ inch of uncut space at the edge. Turn the triangle around and make a parallel cut from the far side, halting again ¼ inch from the edge. Continue making cuts from alternate sides until the triangle's ends have been reached. The closer the cuts, the more delicate the mesh. Carefully unfold the paper and trim away the four dangling ends to form a cobweblike gilded cage.

The paper bird you make to hang inside the cage might be a graceful, white dove or a gay-feathered songster sporting peacock plumage. Light, bright colors stand out best against dark needles. Draw and cut out a bird from a 4-inch square of paper. Enrich your nightingale with flowing tail feathers in rainbow tints, fluffy feathers, a pair of contrasting wings, or a curly topknot. Add ruffled or fringed tissue paper, real feathers, sequins, or glittery sprinkles. Use a needle and thread to suspend the bird within its gilded home. Secure a hanging loop at the top, and the ornament is complete and ready to add a filigreed charm to your holiday decorations.

TREETOP STAR

Stars, symbols of the first Christmas, have twinkled above fragrant green branches since Christmas trees first became a part of the season's celebrations. Victorians topped their lush pyramids of handmade ornaments (or sparkly, store-bought ones) with a perfect, shining, five-pointed star. You can, too, if you follow this simple but precise rule for folding and cutting a flawless star.

Start with a 6-inch square of paper. Fold it in half to form a triangle. Mark the center of the longest side. Place a mark one-third of the way along a short side, then allow the pictures to guide you in making the star's folds. Take care to make a sharp, neat point where folds meet at the bottom and be sure to match edges exactly as in the diagram. Folds must be accurate for perfect results.

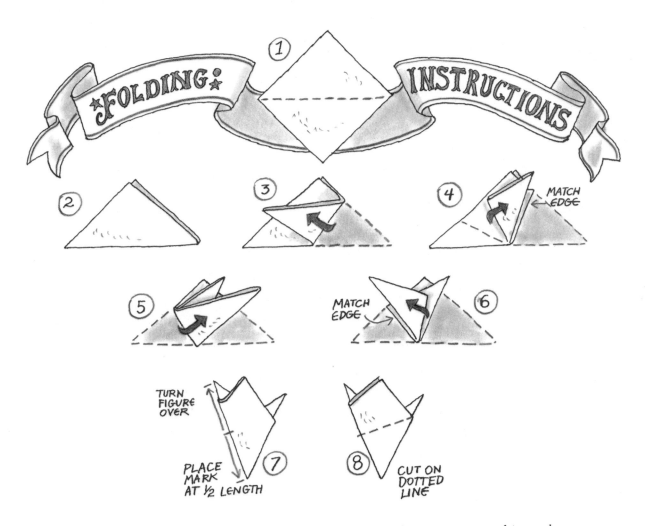

After your star pattern is completed, trace the shape twice onto thin cardboard. (A shirt gift box works well.) Cut out the stars and staple them together around the top points, allowing the bottom to remain open. Use the pattern to make two stars cut from shiny gift wrap or aluminum foil. Use white glue to attach them to the cardboard stars. Slip the bottom opening over the topmost branch of your Christmas tree.

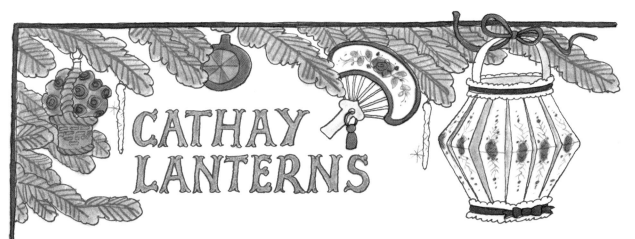

CATHAY LANTERNS

Arts and crafts from distant lands were greatly admired by our forebears. To satisfy the growing vogue for the exotic, clipper ships returned from faraway shores with holds full of these novelties. None of these baubles held more appeal to the Victorian eye than the delicate trifles produced by craftsmen of Cathay. Among these wonders were cleverly folded bits of rice paper which mimicked the shapes of oriental lanterns. These miniatures were often touched with artful flecks of paint that magically suggested dew-fresh cherry blossoms or a light-as-air frolic of butterflies. A silken tassel daintily finished off the trinket.

It was not long before Victorian hobbyists were inspired to try a hand at this age-old paper art. Using the ephemeral dainties as models and adding a dash of very Victorian ruffles and flourishes, they produced a plenitude of light-hearted whimsies that were soon counted part of the magnificent raiment of the parlor Christmas tree.

These surprisingly pretty lanterns can still be easily made from homey supplies. You will need paper, glue, scissors, and trimming scraps from the workbasket or variety store. Contruction paper may be used, but paper with a finer finish will give more elegant results.

Cut a rectangle measuring 2 by 6 inches. Fold the paper in half, lengthwise. Reinforce the crease by pressing with a ruler. Lightly mark the crease every ¼ inch along its length. Cut the paper into strips at these marks, snipping to within ½ inch of the outside edge. Open the paper, and roll it into a cylinder. Overlap the edges slightly,

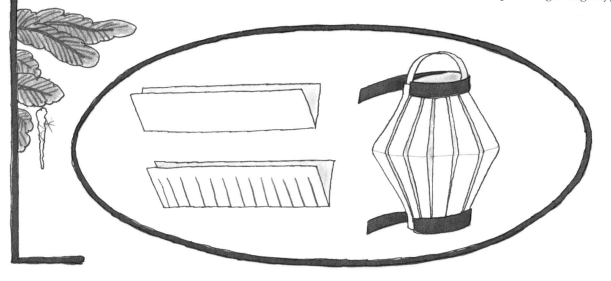

and glue them to form the lantern.

The lantern's edges may be decorated with short pieces of lace, narrow ribbon, metallic cord, beads, or sequins. Bands cut from contrastingly colored paper, fringed or decorated with paint, may also be used; or, wreathe the edges in overlapping, cut-paper leaves and tiny silk flowers. Glue a narrow 7-inch strip of paper inside to the top and bottom bands to help the lantern hold its expanded shape and to serve as a hanger. Add a small tassel made from fine gold cord or satiny embroidery thread, as a Victorian craftsman would have done. Make these Cathay lanterns in several different sizes to add variety to your old-fashioned decorations.

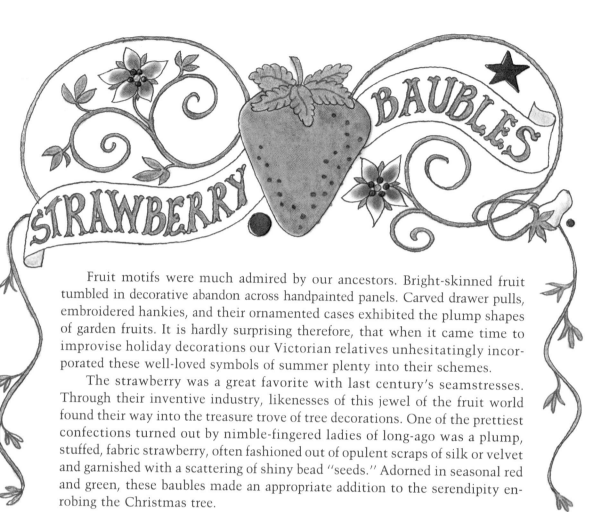

STRAWBERRY BAUBLES

Fruit motifs were much admired by our ancestors. Bright-skinned fruit tumbled in decorative abandon across handpainted panels. Carved drawer pulls, embroidered hankies, and their ornamented cases exhibited the plump shapes of garden fruits. It is hardly surprising therefore, that when it came time to improvise holiday decorations our Victorian relatives unhesitatingly incorporated these well-loved symbols of summer plenty into their schemes.

The strawberry was a great favorite with last century's seamstresses. Through their inventive industry, likenesses of this jewel of the fruit world found their way into the treasure trove of tree decorations. One of the prettiest confections turned out by nimble-fingered ladies of long-ago was a plump, stuffed, fabric strawberry, often fashioned out of opulent scraps of silk or velvet and garnished with a scattering of shiny bead "seeds." Adorned in seasonal red and green, these baubles made an appropriate addition to the serendipity enrobing the Christmas tree.

To make this Christmas fancy you will need scraps of colored fabric with a tendency toward red or green. For red, rosy tints, hot pinks, and brightest scarlets are all acceptable. Silks and velvets constitute the most usual cloths, but woollen and cotton scraps should not be scorned. Examples worked in dainty, blush-pink calico and the jolliest of red and green tartan plaid taffeta are not unknown—the one stipulation being that the piece must accomodate a 7-inch circle. Snippets of leaf-colored fabric, cotton for stuffing, and material for the seed embellishments—be it embroidery floss or tiny beads—should also be gathered.

Cut out a circular pattern approximately 7 inches in diameter. (A dessert plate makes a fine template.) Use the pattern to cut a fabric circle. Fold the circle in half and press along the fold line. Cut the circle in two along the crease. Each semicircle will make a strawberry. Fold the semicircle in two, with the right fabric side turned inward. Stitch along the straight edge. Turn the material right side out and fill the strawberry with cotton batting, leaving enough free fabric to gather in at the top. Close the top edge by drawing in a line of stitches run around the top, carefully enclosing the selvage.

The green calyx crowning the berry can be as ornamental as you care to make it. Cut this topknot from green felt or any other verdant-hued fabric; or, stitch it on in emerald embroidery thread or concoct one out of satiny-sheened ribbon—either looped and pinned down into no-nonsense points, as in one old example, or encouraged in the richly convoluted excesses of a multilooped bow, complete with corkscrew curls and coils.

Seed your bauble with delicate cross-stitches or french knots wrought in silken embroidery floss, or embellish the fruit with light-catching glass beads or spherical-headed dressmaker pins. Add a loop of wool or plaited embroidery thread for a hanger and your strawberry bauble is ready for the Christmas tree.

Before completing the second one to give as a gift, touch its cottony heart with a drop or two of oil of strawberry to bestow the scent of summer on the ornament. (These strawberry shapes also make fine sachets when stuffed with a fragrant jumble of dried flower petals.) Make them by the bowlful—from precious wild strawberry size to giant, pride-of-the-garden size.

❀SNOWBIRDS

Victorian householders displayed great resourcefulness when it came to tree decorations. Limited supplies were no impediment to these ingenious souls. Using the simplest of ingredients, they created pleasing tree decorations. With the natural, snowy world outside their window as inspiration, they concocted airy wonders with only paper, scissors, needle, and thread. Winter birds alighting on the windowsill in search of crumbs, their feathers fluffed against the chill, might have suggested the roly-poly snowbirds that decorated many of last century's trees. Resplendent with beak and wings of gilt paper, this avian delight hung, frozen in midflutter, among the Christmas tree's fragrant boughs.

To make a snowbird, you will need a sheet of lightweight white paper large enough to accommodate a 3-by-24-inch strip and a 1½-by-12-inch strip; silver or gold paper for tail, wings, and beak; black bead-headed pushpins for eyes; scissors; and needle and thread. Cut one strip of white paper of each size mentioned above. Roll each strip into a small cylinder. Fringe both edges of the cylinders, leaving an uncut ¼-inch strip down the middle. Make the fringe as fine as scissors and patience will allow.

Unroll the large strip. Gather the strip along the uncut center with a running line of stitches. Carefully pull the thread to form a fringed body ball. Continuing to stitch with the same length of thread, repeat the

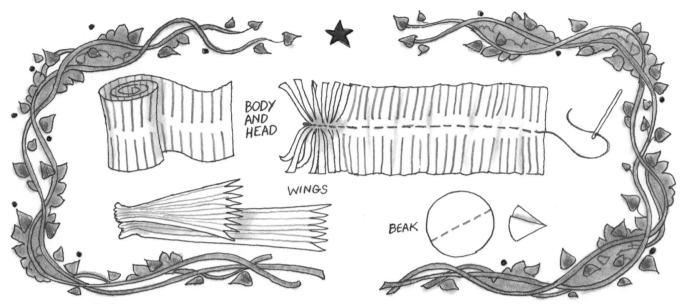

BODY AND HEAD

WINGS

BEAK

gathering with the smaller strip to form the head. Knot and trim the thread. Fluff out the fringe to make a round head and body.

Cut a 2-inch gold paper circle in half, overlapping and gluing one of the semicircles to form a cone. This will serve as the snowbird's beak. Cut two gold rectangles each of 2½ by 3 inches and of 2 by 5 inches for wings and tail. Pleat the rectangles as narrowly as possible, forming long wings and tails. Trim the ends of the folded papers with slanting cuts so that they will be deeply notched or scalloped when opened. Unfold the notched ends of a wing and a tail. Join the still-folded ends with thread and attach them to the body. Attach the remaining wing and tail to the other side.

When the glued beak has dried, sew it to the head. Add black pushpin eyes and a thread or ribbon hanger. Transparent nylon "invisible" thread makes a fine hanger. Arrange the snowbird on a branch tip where it will turn with the slightest air movement.

WOVEN STARS

Using only the simplest of materials, industrious householders managed to array their Christmas trees in splendid assortment. A woven star was one pretty bauble devised by these clever crafters. Although our nimble-fingered ancestors sometimes used paper strips for this intricately folded and twisted ornament, ribbon was preferred. Patience was required to learn the exacting steps, but once these were mastered even the family's younger members could turn out numbers of attractive decorations on long pre-Christmas evenings.

To make a woven star, you will need four strips of paper or ribbon, ¾ inch wide and 24 inches long. For the beginner, ribbon is the best choice. It does not wrinkle as readily as paper and is easiest to work with. Clear, bright colors show off the star's sculptured form to best advantage. Choose ribbon without a right and wrong side. Trim the ends of each length of ribbon to slanting points to facilitate weaving.

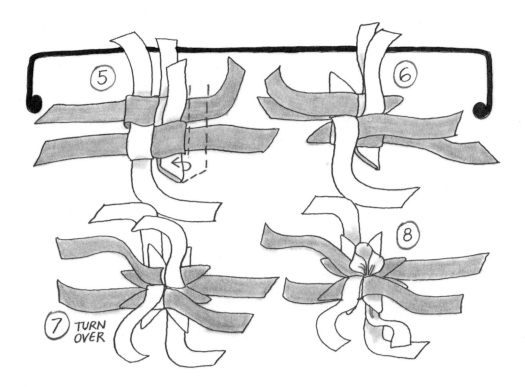

Fold the ribbon pieces in half. Interlock the loops to form a basket weave. Fold the four top ribbons to form a second basket weave on top of the first.

Fold and crease one of the top ribbons as shown in the diagram. Slip its end back through an open side to form a point. Repeat with the three remaining top ribbons to make four star points. Turn the star over. Repeat the folding, creasing, and slipping through open ends to make the other four points.

Make the center standing points by folding back one of the top ribbons. Curl the next strip counterclockwise and slip it into the slit beneath the folded ribbon. Gently pull the ribbon through to form a point. (Care is essential to avoid unraveling the star.) Repeat the process with the remaining top ribbons to form four standing points.

Turn the star over and make four standing points on the other side in the same way. Trim away ribbon ends. Sew on a loop of thread for a hanger.

NUTSHELL DAINTIES

For young Victorians, one holiday fascination was the numbers of dainty homemade gifts decorating the Christmas tree. Senior members of the household spent much time and derived great enjoyment in manufacturing these diminutive wonders of skill and inventiveness. Combining humble materials and elegant scraps, yesterday's craftspeople created a microcosm populated by pocketsized treasures that still engage imaginations of small fry.

Along with charmingly carved and painted menageries, tiny dolls, and assorted furnishings handmade by father in dollhouse proportions, these surprises included exciting gifts-within-gifts—candy morsels, silver thimbles, ribbons, fancy combs, jewelry, and pigmy toys and games that hung concealed in miniature containers. Often, these gift holders began as natural receptacles. Clam shells, milkweed pods, and even birds' nests were utilized, but walnut shells were the most favored of containers. The handicrafter used paint, ribbon, and snippets of silk and lace to convert bits of nature into festive baubles befitting a Victorian Christmas.

Use these dainties as unusual gift wraps or manufacture them only as unique tree decorations. You will need perfect, halved walnut shells and odds and ends of elegant trimmings.

Nutshell Baskets. A lilliputian basket to hold the daintiest of sweets was made from half a walnut shell, fabric, ribbon, and lace scraps. A cardboard handle, covered in narrow ribbon or lace, was glued to the inside of the shell. A small twig was bent to press the handle tightly to the shell until the glue had dried. Later, the inside was lined with an oval of fabric, and lace edging was glued around the basket's rim. Two tiny bows were added where the handle met the basket. These containers held miniature candies or dainty dried flowers. Glossy red berries might be heaped inside before the little basket was added to the host of other ornaments crowding the tree.

Fairy Cradle. This hinged and ribboned walnut held an enchanting surprise for a Victorian miss. When the shell was opened, it revealed an elfin babe nestled in its lacy cradle. The doll might be china or a delicate, painted-wax cherub covered by the tinest of handmade quilts. Sometimes, an incredibly tiny wardrobe accompanied the infant in its nutshell nursery.

To make this Victorian fantasy, drill two holes in each half of a walnut shell. Align the holes to make a back hinge and a front clasp. Line the halves with fabric or silver paper. Glue a frill of lace around the outer edges. Bind the edges with silk ribbon, fixed in place with glue. Snip the ribbon, if necessary, to leave the holes free. Thread a ribbon through the back hinge and join the shells with a bow. Add a small doll or other gift of your choice. If the shell is to be a cradle, you can line the inside edge with another lace strip. Thread another length of ribbon through the clasp and close with a bow and a hanging loop.

SUGAR, SPICE, AND CANDY FRUIT

Christmas has always been a time for feasting, and a Victorian yuletide was no exception. Preparations started as far in advance of the joyous day as the preceding summer, when fruits were candied by long boiling in thick sugar syrups, and concentrated fruit essences, vital to flavoring some extra-special holiday delights, were prepared. In the fall, nuts were squirreled away in burlap sacks and crocks of spicy mincemeat set to cure beside them. As the holiday season approached, from the grocer's came loaves of crystalline sugar, whole spices, and rich chocolate. Tropical fruits—bananas, oranges, and pineapples—rare and expensive in the last century, were purchased as special treats for the coming festivities.

The baking began weeks before the holiday. Every day there were new nose-tingling smells to excite younger members of the household. Streams of cakes, cookies, and candies poured into the already crowded pantry, to be packed away until the celebration began.

You can make some of the same treats that Victorian revelers looked forward to with such relish. Some of these sweets make fine holiday decorations; others are especially fun to make. All are delicious and will add a feeling of times long past to your Christmas celebration.

★ ★ ★

MARZIPAN FRUIT

Who doesn't love the sweet, almondy taste of marzipan? This candy has been a favorite confection for hundreds of years. Shaped into miniature fruits and tinted in a rainbow of realistic tones, it was to be found among the pocket-sized tin toys, diminutive china dolls, and other tiny wonders used to stuff Victorian Christmas stockings. It also appeared among the dazzling finery of old-time Christmas trees,

where miniature marzipan toys filled beribboned "horns of plenty."

To make marzipan candy you will need 1 cup of blanched almonds or canned almond paste, 1 teaspoon of almond extract, 2 cups of sifted confectioner's sugar, and 1 egg white.

Whole almonds must be finely ground. If you use a meat grinder as Grandma would have done, put almonds through the device

three or four times, then mix in the almond extract. You can use a blender or food processor to crush the nuts. Add the extract before you begin, and stop the blender frequently, mixing chopped and unchopped nuts to produce a smooth paste.

Combine the almond paste and sugar. Use another bowl in which to beat the egg whites until they stand in fluffy peaks. Add them to the nut mixture, mix, and knead until the paste is smooth. Add more sugar

or extract, if necessary, to make a firm but not brittle dough.

Break off walnut-sized pieces from the mixture. Shape them to look like pieces of fruit. Carrots and apples are easy; bunches of grapes, harder. Keep the shapes fat and rounded. Leaves can be added, and dots and lines can be modeled with fork tines. Use a small brush and food coloring to tint your fruit in realistic colors. Allow the marzipan to dry overnight before sampling.

After their last sweet notes faded into the starry night, carolers were often asked inside to warm frosted fingers by the crackling yule log. Mugs of steaming punch might be offered the songsters to help vanquish the chill. After emptying the mugs of their spicy contents and offering the host one more wish for a merry Christmas, they trudged on into the crisp night air—the glimmer of oil lamps and distant windows, bright with Christmas candles, leading them to the next round of carols and, they hoped, another warming mug of punch.

Fragrant sweet cider punch, made from an old-fashioned recipe, is just as satisfying today as it was a hundred years ago. Make it for Christmas Eve carolers, serve it to family or friends, or treat yourself to its tangy goodness after a snowy afternoon's sports.

90

You will need 1 quart of apple cider, ¼ cup of brown sugar, a few whole cloves and allspice buds, 1 stick of cinnamon, and a handful of raisins to make a quart of punch.

Heat the cider in a large pot, mixing in the brown sugar and stirring until it is melted. Add the cloves and allspice buds and the stick of cinnamon, along with a generous handful of raisins. Cover the pot and bring the punch just to the boil over high heat. Turn the heat to low and simmer for 15 minutes. Be sure to include a few sweet, plump raisins with each steaming serving.

Ribboning spirals of red and white candy were as much a part of yesterday's Christmas as they are of ours. Unlike today's candy canes, this showy treat was handmade in Victorian times. The candy could be purchased from a confectioner, but some families chose to undertake the job themselves of forming soft taffy into the familiar coiling shapes. Canes are still most successfully assembled with teamwork, so plan this undertaking when you have help.

You will need a candy thermometer, 2 cups of sugar, ½ cup of light corn syrup, ½ cup of water, ¼ teaspoon of cream of tartar, ¾ teaspoon of peppermint extract, and 1 teaspoon of red food color. This will yield about six medium-sized canes.

In a large, heavy-bottomed saucepan, mix the first four ingredients. Stir until the sugar dissolves. Place a candy thermometer

in the mixture. Cook the mixture without stirring until the thermometer registers 265°; then turn off the heat and add the peppermint extract. Divide the mixture in half by carefully pouring part of it into another pan. Add the red food color to one of the pans.

While waiting for the candy to cool enough to allow handling, grease a cookie sheet for each participant, to provide a non-stick working space. Butter your hands, and use a buttered spatula to cut off a portion of the taffy. Have another person do the same with the red taffy. Pull and fold the pieces to a glossy sheen; then roll them each into an 8-inch-long coil. Twist the two coils together, rolling them gently to flatten the colors together. Give the head of the cane a twist before setting it aside to cool and harden on a greased surface.

STAR OF BETHLEHEM

Hard, boiled sugar candies, which come in so many bright colors and fruity flavors, were favorite treats of long-ago Christmases. These crystal-clear candies were sometimes used to make a very pretty goody. On preholiday baking days, when scraps of pastry dough begged to be turned into a special delicacy befitting the festive season, a handful of the rocklike candies would be wrapped in a clean corner of Mother's apron and given a few whacks with a stout rolling pin.

Children were assigned the task of sprinkling the sweet, slivered bits and pieces inside a latticework star formed from strips of the left-over pastry dough. Into the oven it went. Soon tantalizing aromas pronounced it cooked. Out it came—the pastry a flaky, golden brown, and the piles of candy chips melted into bright panes of sweet Christmas candy. Placed in a window, its clear colors glowed like stained glass, but this "glass" was also as tasty as it was pretty.

94

Choose a day when there are left over scraps of pastry to make your star, or follow a simple recipe for pie dough found in most cookbooks. You will need a cup of dough for each star. Roll the pastry into a rectangle wide enough to be cut into five identical strips. Arrange the strips in a star shape on a greased piece of aluminum foil placed on a cookie sheet. Pat where the strips overlap to seal the dough. Wrap a few clear-colored hard candies in a clean, nonfuzzy, kitchen towel and smash them (not too hard!) with a rolling pin or hammer. (Cinnamon fla-vored hard candies smell especially deli-cious when baking.) Fill the open areas be-tween the strips with candy chips. If you use more than one color of candy, separate them to keep melted colors bright and clear. Bake the star in a 400° oven for about 12 minutes or until the candy melts. Over-baking will produce dull, unattractive colors. Wait until your star is cool before peeling away the foil. Make several of these stars so you'll have extra ones to give as gifts and to sample right away.

SWEET HEARTS

Imagine a cookie so light and airy that it disappears almost before you've had a chance to enjoy its sweet lusciousness. That's exactly what happens when you eat an old-fashioned, meringue sweet heart. These brittle puffs of sugary, pink deliciousness were the first cookies to vanish from among the tempting morsels that heaped silver filigreed platters and filled paper doily–lined tins.

To make these airy treats you will need 2 eggs, 8 tablespoons of granulated sugar, 1 teaspoon of vanilla extract, 1 teaspoon orange or almond extract, and a few drops of red food coloring.

Allow the eggs to reach room temperature before separating the whites and yolks into two containers. Use a medium-sized bowl for the whites. Refrigerate the yolks in a small container to use another day.

Beat the egg whites until stiff. Add 6 tablespoons of sugar, beating them in one at a time. Continue beating until the mixture is very stiff and smooth with a gloss like shaving cream. To flavor the sweet hearts, add 1 teaspoon of vanilla and the orange or almond extract. Add a few drops of red food coloring as you mix in the flavorings to tint the mixture a Christmas fairy pink, then fold in another 2 tablespoons of sugar, one at a time.

Divide the frothy cloud into four equal parts, using a rubber spatula. Place one part on each quarter of a greased and floured cookie sheet. Form each of the airy blobs into a heart by pushing the froth out and away from the center. Make the hearts fat or skinny, flat and smooth or covered with peaks and swirls.

The hearts may be decorated with holiday trimmings. Sprinkle the tops with a snow of glittering, colored sugar crystals or outline them with confetti-colored dots or silver balls. Cinnamon hearts will add little red puddles of spicy, melted sweetness.

Set your oven at 250°. Bake the hearts for 1½ hours or until firm to the touch. (If removed sooner they will be chewy instead of meltingly airy.) Allow the hearts to cool before you sample these sweet, light-as-a-feather, melt-in-the-mouth treats.

97

CARAMEL CORN BALLS

That long-time familiar of homey fireside evenings, popcorn, played an important part in yesterday's holiday decorations. Strings of starchy, white kernels looped their way through aromatic branches, taking a place among glittering stars and icicles, beads, berries, and bouquets. The lightly puffed edibles were more apt to attract the younger set's attention, however, if the corn were held together with a sweet, caramelly glue. In fact, the tots probably had a hand in the creation of these spherical delights. Like so many other Christmas preparations, this chore would have been undertaken on one of those lamp-lit evenings that preceded the holiday.

With the first snow ticking at the window, the family gathered around the kitchen table. A senior member prepared the buttery glaze, while eager youngsters juggled the popper on top of the woodstove. The room soon filled with mingling odors of popping corn and buttery steam rising from the caramel pot. When the expanded kernels, laved in sticky dressing, had cooled sufficiently, all hands (lavishly buttered) tackled the sweet task of forming the goo-drenched popcorn into balls. Once hardened and decorated in properly festive trappings, the caramel corn balls were ready to be added to the tree's brilliant array.

To make caramel corn balls you will need 8 cups of freshly popped corn (about 1 unpopped cup), 2 tablespoons of butter, 1¾ cups of brown sugar, 8 tablespoons of water, and a pinch of salt. This will make twelve to fourteen balls.

Melt the butter in a heavy-bottomed saucepan. Add the sugar, water, and salt. Stir the mixture until the sugar dissolves. Bring the mixture to a boil, then lower the heat and cover. Cook the caramel until sugar crystals on the pan sides have melted (about 4 minutes). Remove the lid. Continue to simmer without stirring until a drop of caramel will form a soft ball when dropped into cold water.

Mix the caramel with 8 cups of popcorn. When the corn is cool enough to handle, press it into small snowball shapes with well-buttered hands. Place the balls on a greased cookie sheet to harden.

A circle of netting, gathered in with a bow might have enfolded these chewy decorations, or twists of paper ribbon topped with a multilooped bow prepared them for a spot on the tree. Either way, they made fine additions to the rich and varied trappings of a Victorian Christmas tree.

Plum pudding was the most dramatic dessert of a Victorian Christmas feast, but it was only one of a host of rich morsels that crowded the sideboard. That old favorite, mincemeat, appeared in several appetizing guises among the pies, cakes, and sweetmeats that were elaborately arranged in the best china, cut glass, and silver dishes.

The mincemeat had been prepared by the busy cook at least a month before the festivities. A savory concoction of candied fruits, raisins, apples, lemons, beef, and sugar was laced with a generous helping of brandy, pressed into a crock, and tightly covered. The wonderfully diverse flavors were allowed to meld in the back larder or beneath the cellar stairs until needed for the manufacturing of holiday delicacies. The mincemeat would arrive at the heavily laden board as a steaming, flaky-crusted pie or as a once-a-year cookie treat—mincemeat pouches.

These melt-in-the-mouth, buttery morsels are easily made, now that mincemeat comes from the grocer instead of the

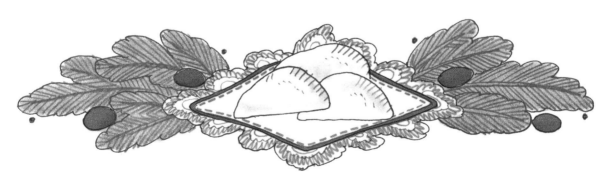

larder. Butter is the flavoring for the crumbly dough; as a result, although margarine may be substituted, taste will be sacrificed if butter is not used. Make the dough ahead of time, since the mixture must be chilled in the refrigerator overnight.

For the cookie dough you will need ½ cup of butter, ¾ cup of sugar, 1 egg, ½ teaspoon of vanilla extract, 1½ cups of flour, ¼ teaspoon of salt, ¼ teaspoon of baking powder, and 1 tablespoon of milk. For the filling, you will need 1 cup of mincemeat and 1 small apple, peeled, cored, and finely chopped. This makes about 24 cookies.

Cream the butter. Add and mix in the sugar, egg, and vanilla. Combine the flour, salt, and baking powder. Mix dry ingredients and milk into the butter mixture. Chill overnight.

For ease in handling, roll only a fifth of the dough at a time. Keep the remainder refrigerated. Use a well-floured board and rolling pin. Cut 4-inch rounds from the dough. (A wide-mouthed jar makes a good stamp.) Arrange the rounds on a greased cookie sheet. Return the gathered scraps to the refrigerator.

Place a teaspoon of the apple-mincemeat mixture on one half of a round. Fold the other half of the round over the filling and seal the edges together with a floured fork. Work quickly so that the buttery dough does not have time to soften.

Bake the pouches in a 400° oven for 10 to 12 minutes until the edges turn a golden brown. These cookies keep their texture better in the freezer than in the cookie jar. Freeze them, and remove as needed.

101

DRUNKEN FRUIT

Lacking refrigeration, Victorian house-holders strove to keep up with cornucopian abundance of summer fruits. The result was pantry shelves crowded with chutneys, pickles, and relishes, along with impressive rows of canned fruits. Some of the finest specimens were set aside with Christmas in mind. Skinned and sliced as needed, the cherries, sweet or tart, blushing peaches, golden apricots, and pears were layered in a capacious crock, sugared, and "drowned" in brandy. This fruit-fancier's delight was allowed to steep in its brandy bath in some dark, cool quarter until the season's celebrations commenced.

At banquet time, the "drunken fruit" arrived in the family's finest cut-glass bowl, to take a place of honor beside a roast goose or turkey. Later, when the celebrators had progressed through the delicious fare, the fruits might appear again, minced into a particularly delectable cake filling, as a piquant accompaniment for some suave pudding, or bejeweling freshly made ice cream. To end the delightful repast and spark a continuation of the merriment, a toast of the heady liquid in which the fruit had steeped might be drunk all around from thimble-sized, light-as-air cordial glasses.

Plan early if you wish to provide your

celebration with this gourmet item. To be at its best the mixture needs to mature for two or three months. The fruit assortment is up to you. A single variety makes a distinctive dish. Sour cherries or peaches are especially good on their own. You might try preparing small containers of different fruits and fruit combinations to discover your favorite.

Choose perfect fruit. Leave short lengths of stem on cherries if they are to be used as a garnish. Prick the fruit a few times with a toothpick. Skin, seed, and slice large fruits, such as peaches, pears, apricots, and pineapples. Weigh the fruit; then layer it in a jar, adding a few peach pits for extra flavor.

Sprinkle on ¼ cup of sugar for each pound of prepared fruit. Add enough unflavored brandy to cover the fruit. (One pound of fruit, ¼ cup of sugar, and ¼ cup of brandy will approximately fill a quart jar.) To stave off the slightest chance of fermentation or spoilage, store the jar in the refrigerator during aging.

Fruit may be added to the mixture at any time. Just be sure to add a complementary amount of sugar and brandy. Let the mixture age sufficiently after the last addition. Less expensive vodka can be substituted for brandy, but the finished product will be quite different in taste (albeit, still in possession of a fruity, drunken zip).

SUGARPLUMS

From Clement C. Moore's well-loved poem "The Night Before Christmas," we all know what kind of visions filled Victorian children's dreams on Christmas Eve. What exactly these sweet morsels were is less common knowledge. Sugarplums are an ancient treat probably originating in the Middle East. There, whole figs were transformed into the original glacé fruit by long and repeated simmerings in a sugary syrup. It was, no doubt, a dish fit for an emir.

Victorians, always ready to gild the lily, shredded the dried sugary fruit along with an assortment of nuts. They mixed this delicious mass with spicy orange rind and exotic crystallized ginger before adding a whiff of that favored seasoning and preservative, brandy. Bite-sized balls of this sticky fruitiness were rolled in sugar and heaped in lacy cornucopias. These "gifts of the Magi" delighted the younger set, and some of the oldsters as well, on Christmas morning.

To make these historical sweets you will need 3 pounds of dried mixed figs, dates, raisins, and currants, 1½ pounds of blanched almonds or walnuts, ½ pound of unsalted, shelled pistachio nuts, ½ pound of crystallized ginger, the grated rinds of 2 oranges, brandy, and granulated sugar. This makes approximately four dozen candies.

Finely chop and mix all ingredients except the brandy and sugar, using a food processor or a food grinder. Add 2 or 3 tablespoons of brandy to make the mixture stick together. Form the mixture into small balls and roll them in sugar. Store the sugarplums in a lightly covered container for a few days while the flavors meld.

The sweet, spicy smell, born in the hot, cast-iron bulk of the cookstove, quickly filled the kitchen. Waves of the delicious odor invaded the dining room, engulfing the broad table and its crisp, fringed cloth and surrounding the crystal prisms of the oil lamp that hung overhead with an aromatic cloud. Skirting the closed doors of the best parlor, it perfumed the front hall and wafted up the stairs. Soon the whole house filled with the nose-tingling aroma. Wherever it greeted them, Victorian children knew this scent of ginger and sugar meant gingerbread—and with gingerbread baking, Christmas couldn't be far off.

Cookies cut from the tangy dough in holiday patterns—stars, bells, wreaths, as well as the familiar shapes of gingerbread

men—were gaily robed and bejeweled with colored icing, raisins, and candied fruit. Christmas Eve found them among other tasty trifles ladening branches of the lavishly bedecked Christmas tree. Why not fill your house with this fine aroma and, in the process, make some delicious Christmas decorations?

You will need ¼ cup of butter, ½ cup of brown sugar, ½ cup of molasses, 3½ cups of flour, 1 teaspoon of soda, ¼ teaspoon of cloves, ½ teaspoon of cinnamon, 1 teaspoon of ginger, ½ teaspoon of salt, and ¼ cup of water. For icing and bejeweling, use ¼ cup of confectioner's sugar, a few drops of water, food coloring, raisins, candied fruit, and fancy cookie decorations. This will make about thirty cookies.

Cream the butter and brown sugar. Add molasses and continue to beat until well-blended. Sift the flour, then resift it with the soda, spices, and salt. Add half of the dry ingredients to the butter mixture and stir well. Blend in the water until the mix-

107

ture is smooth, then add the remaining dry ingredients and mix to make an even dough. If necessary, add more flour to make the dough firm enough to roll.

Roll the dough with a floured rolling pin to cover a greased cookie sheet. Cut out the shapes using a floured cookie cutter, or create your own shapes by cutting paper patterns, laying the pattern on the dough, and carefully cutting around the shape with a knife. When you have filled the sheet with shapes, remove the dough between the cookies to use in rolling and cutting other figures. Poke an opening at the top of each cookie to provide a hole for hanging.

Press in raisins, small pieces of candied fruits, or fancy cookie decorations to make each cookie unique. Bake the gingerbread at 350° for about 8 minutes or until the cookies are firm.

After the cookies have cooled on a cake rack, mix confectioner's sugar with a few drops of water to make a thick, smooth icing. Add a drop or two of food dye if you wish colored icing. Use a knife or toothpick to cover parts of the gingerbread with icing or for making sugary lines. When the icing has hardened, use 12-inch lengths of narrow ribbon to attach your gingerbread cookies to the Christmas tree.

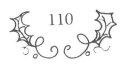